CALIFORNI

ROMANTIC

First published in the
United States of America in 2007 by
RIZZOLI INTERNATIONAL PUBLICATIONS, INC.
300 Park Avenue South
New York, NY
10010
www.rizzoliusa.com

to Dorrie Hall, my visual mentor

The Perfect World

One summer Mom and Dad drove us kids to the San Juan Capistrano Mission to see the swallows come back. I remember standing, late in the afternoon, in front of what looked like an endless row of arches feeling an ache. It seemed to come from my heart. A few months later our family spent a weekend at the Biltmore Hotel in Santa Barbara. Mom said we were going to sleep in a 1920s Spanish building where movie stars such as Cary Grant used to stay. Even though I was a girl, I remember the dark wood beamed ceiling in the lobby. It looked like it reached the stars and beyond; that's how high it was. I remember the coolness inside set against the heat outside. Shadow and light. Inside and out. It was a world of opposites. A perfect world. That was the summer it came to me: the idea that beauty could be felt from standing in the glow of afternoon light reflected on the colonnade of a mission. That's when I came to understand that the ache of romance lived within the walls of our Spanish heritage.

Ten years ago there was an old Spanish Colonial Revival house for sale on Roxbury, north of Sunset. The broker called it "tear down." I saw neglect, but felt Beauty. I bought it. I restored it. My family and I lived in it. A few years later I found another Spanish home. We bought it, restored it, and lived in it. The ache of a girl had become the obsession of a woman.

California Romantica is the outcome of that obsession. As with most obsessions, I had many expectations. I knew I wanted to share the magic I'd felt within the aura created by the presence of Spanish architecture in Southern California. I knew I wanted to help articulate a different way of appreciating what Wallace Neff referred to as "California Homes for California People." I wanted to capture the romance of an empty room. I wanted to focus on details, a fountain, a staircase, a doorway. I wanted to highlight the genre's disjointed symmetry, and informal abstract appeal. I wanted the drama of light to reveal secrets that lay hidden beyond the facades. I wanted "Old" and "Spanish" to stop being code words for demolition. I wanted us to give renewed vitality, and even a refined Modernism, to the historic dream of living in a perfect California Spanish home.

Maybe what's so appealing about the imperfect world of the California Spanish home is its startling juxtapositions. Such a house unveils an evocative past while offering at the same time the promise of a hope-filled future. This is wonderfully seductive. One is at once assured of security in cool shaded patios, and yet, set against the vast expanse of an uncertain world, one is kept on one's toes. Dense archways guide us to shadowed arcades that lead to blinding light. Courtyard living underscores the intensity of black iron grills that frame white stucco walls that are topped off by red tile roofs. Out of this alluring opposition comes a fantasy of heaven.

The promise of heaven in a home lies somewhere out there, almost within reach. It resides in a place mapped by the history of our longings. When I think of home I see a giant bulletin board thumb-tacked with hundreds of thousands of photographs, plastered across the panorama of my mind. Over the years, the images that refuse to disappear are those that center on the beauty of Spanish architecture. It's almost as if they remain to remind me of something I've long known, but haven't always acknowledged, something sensed deep down and from as far back as the day I felt that ache standing in front of the San Juan Capistrano Mission 50 years ago.

Today the ache doesn't come from the heart of the girl who used to be me. It isn't driven by longing. It isn't propelled by a desire to own a home from the perfect world. Today the ache hovers over an encroachment of loss. Believing our *Residencias De Grande* will endure as long as there are people left to inhabit them doesn't go far in the world of action. Proving that California's indigenous Hispanic architecture conforms to a modern lifestyle isn't enough. To be an effective advocate takes more than that. All I know is that somehow somebody or something has to jump-start our community into making an effort to save from extinction the legacy of George Washington Smith, Wallace Neff, Lillian Rice, Joseph Plunkett, Arthur Kelly, Paul Williams, and their less recognized architect colleagues.

So, here they are. twenty homes from the perfect world for you to see. Here they are, presented with love and respect in anticipation that you too will feel the ache of their romance. Here they are, in honor of California's rich Arts and Crafts tradition. Here they are, offered in tribute to the owners and collectors and designers and architects who brought them into the light of our gaze. Here they are, with their stories, their magic, their whims, their charm, their mistakes, and their essence intact. Here they are, our Mission, Andalusian, Monterey, Hacienda, Land-grant, Estancia, Rancho, Spanish homes. Here they are, offered in hopes that they will fulfill that secret wish for the ambiguity of dreams, the dark side of romance, and the bittersweet lie of perfection.

Diane Keaton

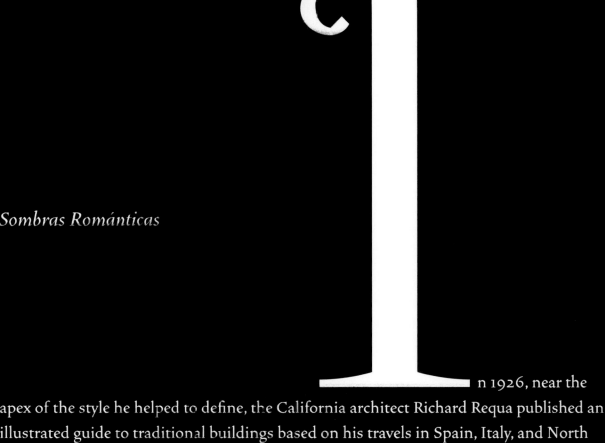

Sombras Románticas

I n 1926, near the
apex of the style he helped to define, the California architect Richard Requa published an
illustrated guide to traditional buildings based on his travels in Spain, Italy, and North
Africa. Requa's book has the imposing—and truly thorough—title: *Architectural Details.
Spain And The Mediterranean. A Portfolio Of One Hundred And Forty-Four Plates; Reproductions
Of Photographs Taken, Selected And Arranged Especially For Use In Developing A Logical And
Appropriate Style Of Architecture For California And The Pacific Southwest.*

Requa's travels were driven by a booster's zeal for an idea of home in California.
"[T]he main reason for the rapidly increasing interest in the western Mediterranean
countries," he wrote in the portfolio's introduction, "is the growing appreciation of the fact
that the logical, fitting, and altogether appropriate architecture for California and the
Pacific southwest is a style inspired and suggested by the architecture of those countries."

Arches, towers, balconies, patios, terraces, window grills, tile work, and stout
doors with metal bosses were elements of this style (and not unique to Requa). But it would
be a mistake to believe that only the exotic details mattered to the men (and some women)
who incorporated tile, stucco, wrought iron ... and sunlight and shadow ... into the homes
that well-to-do clients commissioned. The romantic houses of the Spanish Colonial Revival
had a calculated modernity, too.

Requa—like Wallace Neff, George Washington Smith, Joe Plunkett, Lillian Rice,
and other California architects at the turn of the twentieth century—wanted to house
imaginations. The golden light pouring into the houses they designed (and into their
room-like gardens and patios) was part of a larger conception of life in the West. The light
beckoning from terraces and tower windows was part of that conception, too; the
imagination is illuminated by Californian sunlight, they believed, and the enlightened
imagination dispels the darkness.

We may think of them as only nostalgic, but houses in Spanish Colonial Revival style are as much of the future as of the past. Their owners and their architects sought a perfect confluence of place and dwelling that would, they thought, redeem modern life from its addictions to speed and anxiety. Nearly a century later, the houses still remind us that utopian aspiration was important to Californians at the start of the twentieth century. After all, every house is the template for a life.

Mission Style

By the late 1880s, the domestic templates of the Gilded Age and the École des Beaux Arts wore poorly for some Californians who were attempting to incorporate the character of the California landscape into their habits of living. The Arts and Crafts movement in its many forms—as architecture, furnishings and decoration—suggested escape through a "higher provincialism." For these Californians, a refined provincialism came to mean an acceptance of what was both commonplace and alien—the Hispanic and Catholic heritage of the Pacific Coast and the desert Southwest. Acceptance was imperfect and partial—living in a house that imitated a colonial-era mission or a Navajo pueblo did not make anyone any less segregationist or anti-Catholic. Still, the blending of cultures—and the beginning of new habits—must start some place. Perhaps it is in a room where New Spain (and not New York or Chicago or Paris) tempers the rhythms of everyday life.

The Mission style—where the Spanish Colonial Revival begins—was California's unique expression of Arts and Crafts ideals: simple, indigenous, traditional, and available. Between 1888 and 1918, the Mission style was adapted to train stations, theaters, hotels, public libraries, government buildings, and a few homes in California, Arizona, and Texas. The style did not seek to replicate a specific building type (much less a specific eighteenth-century mission church). Its elements, drawn from the adobe architecture of the Spanish and Mexican colonial frontier, were intended only to be impressionistic. Scalloped and recurved gable ends (called *espadañas*), low towers composed of diminishing squares, shallow domes, pan tile roofs, thick pilasters, and broad spans of roughly stuccoed or plastered wall set a mood—specifically the elegiac mood of Helen Hunt Jackson's wildly popular novel *Ramona* (published in 1884).

The Mission style—sober and largely undecorated—could be made more appealing as "Hispano-Moorish" with the addition of horseshoe arches (often supported by clusters of pillars), elaborate tiling patterns, filigreed metalwork, and low fountains in entry courtyards. Or it could be made a kind of "provincial Baroque" through the application of Churrigueresque terracotta castings to doorways and window surrounds. The Mission style provided only a narrow range for this kind of eclecticism, however. Some called the style too puritan and too primitive.

And one architect from this early period—Irving Gill—extended the style far beyond the frontier of Craftsman ideals to pure form: straight line, arch, cube, circle, and rectangular surface. Gill's mature work between 1900 and 1919 stripped away applied details to reveal with startling frankness the fundamental structural units of his buildings. Gill's rigorous abstraction, which made a Californian connection between the Craftsman movement in America and the emerging modernists in Europe, was widely praised but less widely accepted.

Ultimately, the Mission style faltered after World War I because of the growing connoisseurship of architects and the greater sophistication of their wealthy clients. In seeking the assurance of educated taste in the design of their homes, both architect and client turned to a new library of photographic guides to traditional European buildings and their structural details. In many cases, both client and architect also had direct experience of the subtle harmonies of traditional houses and their landscapes through extensive travels in Spain, Italy, the south of France, and North Africa.

California Style

The starting point for the second phase of the Spanish Colonial Revival in California is generally set at San Diego's Panama California International Exposition of 1915. Bertram Goodhue's insistence that the Mission style was inappropriate for the important buildings at the fair announced the transition from Mission to Mediterranean, but it was less a declaration of a new building style and more an example of adroit marketing for the newly professionalizing practice of architecture. The example of the colonial and Native American architecture of California, Arizona, and New Mexico, still present in their surviving eighteenth- and early-nineteenth-century buildings, was insufficient. Revivalist homes and commercial buildings, the exhibition made clear through its scholarly eclecticism, would require the skills of a widely traveled, well read, and distinctly modern professional designer.

Colonial Mexico, the capitals of South America, the rural villas of southern France and Italy, the town houses of Morocco and Tunisia—even Persia—offered not only a greater exoticism and a wider range of building types but also a maximal mixing of cultural elements across a longer history. The pivot of the hybridizing California imagination, not surprisingly, was Spain—specifically the Spain of *al-Andalus* under its Moorish caliphs between the eighth and fifteenth centuries and Spanish Andalusia after 1500. Much has been said about the symmetry of climate and landscape in Andalusia and California—it was practically all that was said about California at the start of the twentieth century—and these shared elements readily supported a romanticized (and heavily Anglicized) vision of harmony between place and people. But there was a suggestion of something more in spirit of the Spanish Colonial Revival, something of the Mudéjar admixture of Islamic, Sephardic, and Gothic cultures and peoples. The authority of early Modernism would ignore the possibilities for cultural complexity in the Spanish Colonial Revival, even as modernist architects extolled the virtues of California's sunlight and freedom. But between 1916 (the date of George Washington Smith's iconic first home) and 1931, the architects who worked in the mixed Mediterranean style would design whole cities of houses of such astonishing sympathy and presence that they continue to be the common memory of what many Californians call home.

Who were the architects who assembled the elements of a hugely popular building style from such heterogeneous materials? They were, first of all, George Washington Smith of Santa Barbara, Wallace Neff of Pasadena, Richard Requa of San Diego, John Byers, Gordon Kaufman, Arthur Kelly, and Paul Williams of Los Angeles, Lillian Rice of Rancho Santa Fe, Lutah Maria Riggs of Montecito, and followed by a great many more—Joe Plunkett, James Osborne Craig, Reginald Johnson, Ronald R. Coates, Elmer Grey, William Templeton Johnson are only a few of the better known. They designed houses for a knowing clientele of successful businessmen and their wives (often seeking semi-retirement in California) who wanted modern household conveniences, accommodation for their automobiles, access to outdoor amenities, rooms that flattered their taste but with an appealing modesty, and houses that spoke to their longing to be connected to California (even if that connection was largely an invented one).

As David Gebhard noted in 1967 in his article "The Spanish Colonial Revival in Southern California" in the *Journal of the Society of Architectural Historians*, "these designers produced buildings that were conceived of as sculptural volumes, closely attached to the land, whereby the basic form of the building was broken down into separate, smaller shapes, which informally spread themselves over the site. Detailing, both within and without, was simple; and the number of materials employed was severely limited."

Within their limited range of materials, the architects of the Spanish Colonial Revival managed a diversity of solutions to the problem of making a home in California, often in the form of fully planned communities—Rancho Santa Fe, San Clemente, and Palos Verdes Estates—and older communities that adopted the Mediterranean style as a planning model—Ojai and post-earthquake Santa Barbara. Human-scaled, in touch with the landscape, and narratively coherent, these neighborhoods showed how unforced historicism and domesticated modernity might be successfully joined. The Depression ended that project. The "California style" in housing and town planning, which depended on well-to-do clients and a particular set of values was over, except in a diminished afterlife as a tract house look for square miles of suburban neighborhoods—stucco, tile trim, a flat roof, and a cement figure of a sleeping Mexican on the porch.

Between its rise and devolution into mediocrity—in less time than the careers of some its practitioners—the Spanish Colonial Revival gave California a distinct architectural vocabulary, a habit of indoor and outdoor living, a playfulness that signaled something new about domesticity, a new tradition in landscape design, and a body of well-wrought town plans, public places, and houses.

They were houses of white stucco and red tile ... of deeply recessed doorways, windows, and portals ... of rustic field tiles and rudely forged iron ... of sunny gardens and shaded corners ... of airy loggias and quiet arcades leading into the light. They were reserved (at least the best of them) but joyful houses that promised delight. They were houses for a Californian imagination.

Romantic Shadows

Californians at the turn of the twentieth century were mythologizers and romanticizers, but we still live in the houses they willed into being. We still long for the landscapes they first saw. We try to see, as they did, how the play of light and dark on a plain white wall engages the built world with nature's world. We handle the domestic things they smoothed with their repeated touch as if to renew a lost connection to them. We pass through the rooms they inhabited knowing that we must be a future owner's shadowed companions one day. We desire all these intimacies, and these houses generously reveal them.

Our own house and garden may be all that we will ever know intimately of beauty, form, and design. It will be the only place where we have knowledge of what lies behind every door, where every shadow is inhabited. As the architect and historian Witold Rybczynski noted in *Home: A Short History of an Idea*, "To speak of domesticity is to describe a set of felt emotions, not a single attribute. Domesticity has to do with family, intimacy, and a devotion to the home, as well as with a sense of the house as embodying—not only harboring—these sentiments. Not only (is) the interior a setting for domestic activity— as it had always been—but the rooms, and the objects that they contained, now acquired a life of their own. This life was not, of course, autonomous, but existed in the imagination of their owners, and so, paradoxically, homely domesticity depended on the development of a rich interior awareness." Or as Gaston Bachelard said (in *The Poetics of Space*), "The house is one of the greatest powers for the integration of the thoughts, memories, and dreams of mankind."

Diane Keaton, who knows the houses of the Spanish Colonial Revival as few do, reminds us that all houses have a shaping power over our dreams of a moral life. If that belief, which I share, is romantic, then the houses in the pages that follow are romance embodied and embraced.

The world is hard to live in, it seems to me, and we need allies. Your house can be a hero, too. And how else could it ever be home, if you did not fall in love with it?

D. J. Waldie

THE
FRENCH
RANCH

L

ight. Then air and earth. Followed by shelter and, inevitably, by memory. Southern California's plains and hills were presented to each wave of enchanted occupiers from the eighteenth century to our own in the same sequence of revelations and reactions. You can replay the marvelous pageant back through memories of Californian houses to the houses themselves, as they still persist. You can step through their deeply set doorways into shaded gardens from which a vista of brown hills and distant lavender mountains rests in the golden light. Perhaps everything in that scene has suffered some change, but memory and that light remain. And when recollection fades, there will still be the light.

Homes in the style that has come be called Spanish Colonial Revival, like the recently rebuilt French Ranch in the Conejo Valley northwest of Los Angeles, take light as their essential building material.

They take the light, reflect it, admit and attenuate it, accept its defining touch on every surface, and they endure it. The dialog between such light and such houses has a long history, from the masters of California revivalist architecture—George Washington Smith, Wallace Neff, Lillian Rice, Richard Requa, Arthur Kelly Reginald Johnson, Myron Hunt, John Byers, Lutah Maria Riggs, Gordon Kaufmann, Roland E. Coate, Joseph Plunkett, among them—through the domestic structures of the American Southwest in the nineteenth century to the Mexican and Spanish colonial periods in California and, by appropriation, the villas and farmhouses of Andalusia, Tuscany, and North Africa ... wherever the light cuts knife edges of shadow on walls of ochre, taupe, faded blue and green, and brilliant white.

The French Ranch is one such memory. It faithfully recalls an earlier house on the site, designed by the noted Santa Monica architect John Byers (best known for his many residential commissions in Brentwood, Pacific Palisades, and Bel Air). That house was razed after a fire destroyed a bedroom and the library. In its place—and on the footprint of the original house—a new version was built that preserves the outline of the Byers design while expanding the living space inside. The result is not a recreation of the vanished house but a collaboration with the idea of the Byers original—a *hacienda* in the relaxed manner of the Spanish southwest with a long, arcaded facade, substantial courtyard gateway, and cool interior passages. That style of house, suited to the demands of frontier ranch life, was typically a single story of connected rectangular rooms with thick

adobe brick walls for protection from the summer sun. In the French Ranch, white plastered walls penetrated by circular arches and deeply inset windows similarly modulate the brightness of noon light. What is distinctive is the massive, barrel vaulted corridor through the house from entry to courtyard fountain. Beneath is an intricately tiled floor that changes in pattern from room to room in a play of colors and reflected light. More tiles ascend the wide stairs to the second floor, ornament the floors and walls of the master bath, and crown an astonishing kitchen ceiling.

Grand and yet not too grand. On the corridor's walls run a row of pegs from which would have hung, if this were the home of a wealthy *Californio* of the mid-nineteenth century, ristas of dried peppers, *chaparajos* to be worn by a rider in the dense chaparral of the foothills, sliver mounted bridles and halters, and lariats of finely braided leather. That past—of lordly men on horseback and women in silk shawls embroidered in Manila—is evoked by the French Ranch, but also the past of twentieth-century Californians who dreamed in the 1920s of men on horseback. Californians then thought that the horsemen's place might belong to them if their new homes in the Spanish Colonial Revival style projected their owners into a landscape of sunlight and shadow.

All houses are in some fashion time machines.

LOS
PAVOS
REALES

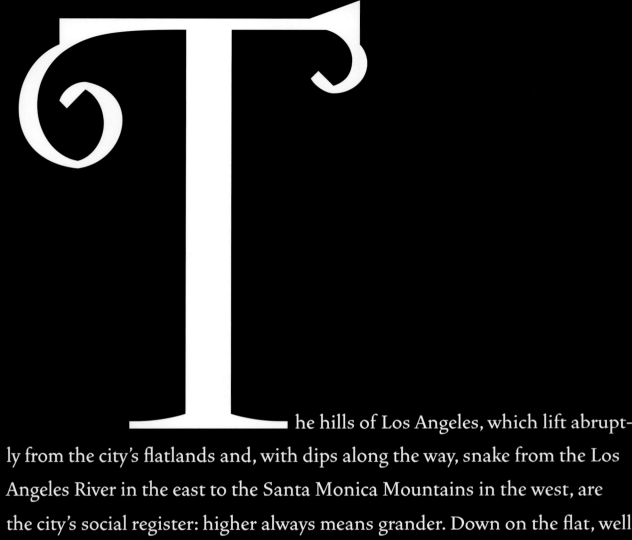

The hills of Los Angeles, which lift abruptly from the city's flatlands and, with dips along the way, snake from the Los Angeles River in the east to the Santa Monica Mountains in the west, are the city's social register: higher always means grander. Down on the flat, well into the twentieth century, meant living with the threat of periodic flooding (hundreds drowned in Los Angeles and nearby communities in the floods of 1934 and 1938). In the modest foothills, streets of middleclass bungalows climbed partway into better neighborhoods. From above them—on the greater slopes of Los Feliz, Hollywood, Beverly Hills, and Brentwood—the estates of the wealthy looked down. In the mid-1920s, booming Los Angeles was busy sidestepping westward and upward into fashionable hillside subdivisions where big lots were built on by new owners flush with movie,

manufacturing, banking, and department store money. The city's most stylish architects followed them.

The Drucker House on Cockerham Drive in Los Feliz, designed by Wallace Neff, represents one side of the city's vertical ambitions. Neff was, perhaps unfairly, pegged as merely "operatic" after his first commissions in Los Angeles drew so much attention that "Wallace Neff" quickly became a much imitated style all its own. This house, built around 1926 (and remodeled by Neff in 1934), has many of the features of that style, but they are restrained and well proportioned. The pan tile roofs of the L-shaped wings are as nearly flat as those of Neff's Ojai Valley Country Club. Window grills (by Julius Dietzmann) are gridded into ribbon loops and topped by crests. The chapel-like entry flanked by miniature towers and finials is a form Neff also reused. The tall drum of the entry hall suggests the tower that Neff employed as counterpoint to the rectangular facades of his houses. Except that assertive and idiosyncratic tower is missing here (because this had once been the rear of the house). Instead, the reoriented Drucker House greets the visitor chastely, with a simplicity enforced by the new entry's Doric columns, plain arch, and mostly unadorned doorway.

It's the entry door grill that undercuts the churchly. Scrolled into wide spirals, its metalwork (with variations on other door grills) probably gave the house its sometime name: *Los Pavos Reales* / The Peacocks. That may be the only thing preening about this door, though. Cutout dogs (a signature motif of Deitzmann's metal work) guard the entry, suggesting the kind

of mid-1920s whimsy that Neff and his clients enjoyed. The tension in Neff's work is often at this level—between the grand and the charming.

Beyond the sunny courtyard, through the circular entry, and past deep arches are rooms that suggest stage sets more than living spaces, as if they were perpetually waiting for a knot of well-dressed men and women to enter. They will, after a drink and some movie industry conversation, leave for an evening of dinner and dancing. The plain walls, conventionalized Spanish-style motifs, and air of expectancy are backdrops for lives that are seemingly being lived elsewhere. Neff's designs, even the most accomplished ones, often appear to be open-ended in this way. They do not seek to establish a rapport with the landscape or make general claims about what a house in California ought to be. They are not arguments; they are purer assertions of the imagination than that.

The style of *Los Pavos Reales* is just a style, carried out with skill and restraint. But houses, unlike stage sets, are planted in a muddle of circumstances, not built on a soundstage. Daylight, not Klieg light, falls on houses in Los Angeles. In the fall months, the city's liquid, golden light upends the detachment a house might possess. The light of Los Angeles fills volumes. Here, it makes playful silhouettes populate empty rooms in a house that had been made for peacocks.

STABLES

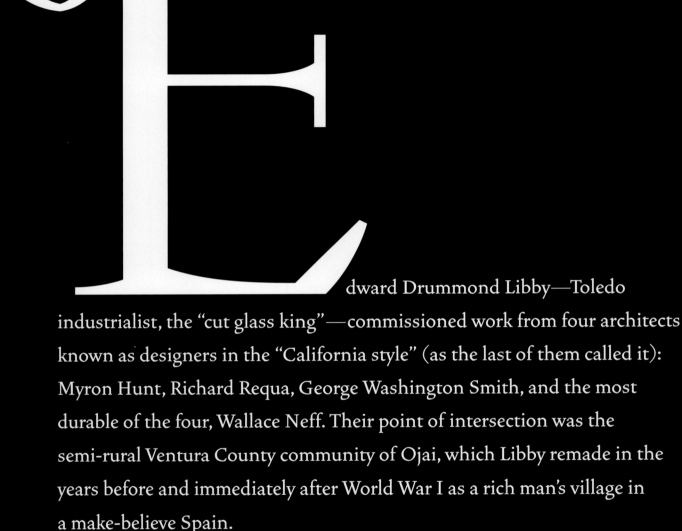

E dward Drummond Libby—Toledo industrialist, the "cut glass king"—commissioned work from four architects known as designers in the "California style" (as the last of them called it): Myron Hunt, Richard Requa, George Washington Smith, and the most durable of the four, Wallace Neff. Their point of intersection was the semi-rural Ventura County community of Ojai, which Libby remade in the years before and immediately after World War I as a rich man's village in a make-believe Spain.

Libby was charmed by the twenty-seven-year-old Neff (as all of Neff's clients tended to be over the next fifty years) and commissioned from him two projects in 1923: the Ojai Valley Country Club—which Neff rendered as ground hugging and nearly flat-roofed—and a cow barn and stables on Libby's "Arbolada" estate. It wasn't the stylish clubhouse that made Neff's youthful reputation; however, it was his remarkable barn.

In the draftsman's elevations, the west facade of the building suggests rural Normandy: a flat-fronted, two-story barn, shingled rather than tiled, with low wings appended on either end, the wing on the right anchored by a squat tower with an entry of parabolic arches that seem to spring out of the ground. The tower might have been designed by someone who had just come back from the Crusades. The east face of the building shows a rough-hewn gallery reached by an exterior stair and two wings enclosing a farmhouse yard suggestive of the Monterey style that followed the American occupation of California in 1847.

In reality, this assemblage of shapes and surfaces was not intended to imitate any style or place. It suggests only the whimsical. Neff would make a long career out of delighting his clients with equal vivacity and imagination.

Neff's barn of many parts made a splash, illustrated (with actual cows attending) in architectural magazines that noted the barn's fashionable eclecticism and its unplastered adobe construction (the exposed bricks treated to prevent erosion). It was like nothing ever built in colonial California. With its unexpected distortions, unusual arches, and diminutive gates (one sporting silhouettes of a dog and hissing cat), the barn was firmly in the architectural tradition of a "folly." It was a real enough enclosure for cows and horses, tack and hay, but it had been built primarily to amuse. In the barn's cheerful disregard for authenticity lay some of the seeds of Disneyland and Las Vegas.

When the property was acquired from Libby's widow by William Lucking in 1927, he turned to another young Ojai architect, Austen Pierpont, to remake the barn and stables into an equally idiosyncratic home with the addition of servants' quarters and a garage. The barn-turned-home—with its rusted-iron hardware, whitewashed and roughly replastered garden walls, and wood dark with rain and sun—has long since weathered into its place.

Inside, the living room (its extra height once meant for hay storage) is bracketed at one end by a characteristically deep fireplace and at the other by a wide loft reached by a stair that springs in the form of another parabolic arch. Hand-wrought ironwork (much of it said to have been made in the smithy on the property) latches doors and windows, forms railings, and curls into a grand chandelier. Another fireplace anchors the wing Pierpont redesigned. Deep enough almost to be another room, the vast fieldstone fireplace and its wide hearth seem more Adirondack than Southern Californian.

Houses generally are accretions. Like stories told many times to different audiences, they gain additions and endure editing. Given time and enough lives, no house is original. Like Neff's cow barn—a blaze of imagination for a mundane purpose—the best architecture shrugs off the question of authenticity as the decades pass. Are the mottling of the stonework, the rusted iron, and the worn adobe not authentic? And when light pours from a welcoming door and shadows gather beneath the heavy branches of an oak, are they not original with the house and forever new?

RAVENSCROFT

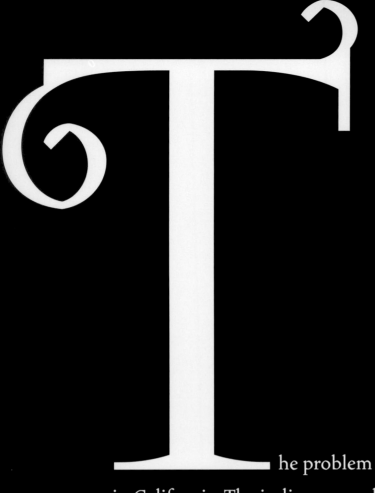

he problem was—and still is—how to make a home in California. The indigenous adobes of dusty Los Angeles and Santa Barbara were, at best, simple rectangular blocks of rooms. Into these low, dim spaces a doorway offered entrance, two or three wood-shuttered windows provided ventilation, and the ubiquitous red field tiles covered what had once been a floor of packed dirt. No one among the waves of Anglo immigrants who arrived after 1870 would have called that kind of house a home, no matter how romantic it may have looked drooping with roses and bougainvilleas.

The search for an acceptable and usable past, for a past that *ought to have been*, occupied the brief and brilliant career of George Washington Smith. Between 1919 and 1930, with the help of Lutah Maria Riggs (who drafted many of his sketches into buildable designs), Smith completed fifty-four Santa Barbara and Montecito houses. All were hybrids. Provincial Spain, Morocco, ancient Persia, Tuscany, Mexico, the south of France, and even something of the distained adobes—Smith worked these traditions into a mixed style that was loosely called Mediterranean.

His wealthy clients could be demanding, even eccentric. Mrs. Geoffrey Stuart Courtney (later, Mrs. Ravenscroft) had endured the San

Francisco earthquake and fire. She wanted a house of concrete and steel. She wanted a house that would shelter against almost any contingency. In 1922, Smith improvised for her an H-shaped floor plan with two wings separated by a long, wide living room. It has a sloping, shed-like ceiling that rises over a walk-in fireplace surmounted by a monumentally abstract double staircase.

Smith had seen and felt the "shock of the new" in pre—World War I France and Italy. Like Irving Gill, his contemporary, Smith was busy domesticating modern Cubist geometry in Ravenscroft even as he sought to evoke an imagined past. The seemingly random planes of the rooflines that gather around the central tower of Ravenscroft recall Paul Cézanne's views of Mont St. Victoire more than the roofline of a Spanish farmhouse.

Ravenscroft asserts, with the authority of Modernism, that space alone can signify as much as surfaces can, that a room might be defined as a certain volume of interior light. Fancywork in wrought iron and leaded-glass stars, the commonplaces of pantile roofs and window grills, even the calculated exterior views that seem to locate the house in Tuscany are more applied than essential to the plan of Ravenscroft. The corner fireplaces are as formal as fragments of a sculpture by Henry Moore. It's a house seeking a way home through abstraction.

The balance between charming detail and Smith's knowingly modern idea of space tipped differently in Ravenscroft than at other, later houses he designed. Before his career abruptly ended in 1930, he firmly turned to designing houses that took a similar pleasure in mass and volume.

A circle of wrought iron daggers blocks opposing occuli over the paired flights of steps to the second floor. Their light animates the plastered walls stretching away on either side, matching the downward slope of the ceiling. Ellipse, rectangle, circle, wedge. Black, white, gray. Something large and simple is gathering shape in this room.

OJO
DEL
DESIERTO

*actus blossoms of flaming coral, velvet spears of in-
digo bushes, misty smoketrees of pinkish pearl, and palos verdes of apple green.*

Ojo del Desierto, 1928

Ojo del Desierto—Eye of the Desert—is a poetic name for a garden in
a wasteland. Palm Springs at the start of the twentieth century qualified: a
stand of indigenous desert fan palms, the famous hot springs, and a few
makeshift buildings surrounded by a vast emptiness. But early Palm Springs
soon found its aficionados, its heat seekers with a fondness for bare rock,
cactus, and endless sky. By the mid-1920s, Palm Springs had grown from
desert outpost to winter playground and acquired a resort hotel and its first
luxury homes. Among the earliest was the house built on a ledge above
the grounds of the Desert Inn for Long Beach oilman Tom O'Donnell and
his wife.

The *Ojo del Desierto* was designed in 1925 by W. C. Tanner and
completed barely in time for the winter season of 1926. Writing in *The House*

Beautiful magazine in 1928, Mary Kellogg was almost giddy from her precipitous climb up to the O'Donnell House from the desert floor (it was the highest house in Palm Springs for nearly forty years). The house itself was dreamlike: "The adobe walls have been colored a greenish gray to match the stony slopes," Kellogg marveled, "the woodwork has been blackened to match the shadows, and the tiles of the roof are stained pink to match the sunset glows." She concluded, perhaps too easily, that it was a "pervading sense of unreality" that invested the Eye of the Desert with its startling character.

Kellogg also noted the eccentricities of a house that was not really meant for everyday living. The kitchen was tiny. The O'Donnells and their guests took their meals at the bottom of the mountain at the Desert Inn. The house was so open to the desert that it was more for shade than anything else. Nearly every room opened out to the valley below or the mountain above. The bedrooms were mere sleeping porches with dressing rooms attached. The flat roof of one block of rooms, far above nosey neighbors, was for sunbathing.

When Kellogg visited the house, the O'Donnells had furnished it with tapestries, vividly colored pottery, Navajo rugs, and a few antique pieces from Mexico and Spain. Native palm trees, brought up from Tahquitz Canyon, framed the entry courtyard at the end of the long, steep drive. To Kellogg, the house, its decoration, and the setting were intimately connected, their textures and colors blending inside and out seamlessly.

The *Ojo del Desierto*, after many alterations and more recent restoration, still commands a remarkable vista from its perch over the city. And if Palm Springs is far larger now and greener and more conventionally suburban than it was in the mid-1920s, it takes only a glance at the blue, purple, and rose of the bare San Jacinto Mountains in the distance to reconnect with the O'Donnells' affection for their *Ojo del Desierto*, their house of repose in a wasteland. Its solitary presence is still framed with desert rock, the spines of ocotillo and agave, the parchment white of yucca blossoms, and the fire of bougainvilleas in bloom. The modest, spare rooms still reside coolly beneath Spanish tile roofs by day, their corner fireplaces promising warmth on a midwinter night. And the adjacent ravine of the cactus garden, laid with flat stones and a pattern of cobbles, still clings to the slope.

The house defies easy categorization. Part Monterey style with its second floor gallery, part Spanish Revival with its great hooded fireplace, part plain adobe hacienda, and with something of the O'Donnells' own idiosyncratic embrace of the aesthetics of the desert, this house is a hybrid of many times, places, and affections. When the changing weather whites out the valley sprawl below, when a full moon lights the heights above, when the visitor, from a shaded corner of a room, contemplates a wall of shattered boulders hanging from the mountain ledge, the *Ojo del Desierto* wraps itself again in mystery.

GUERRA
ESTATE

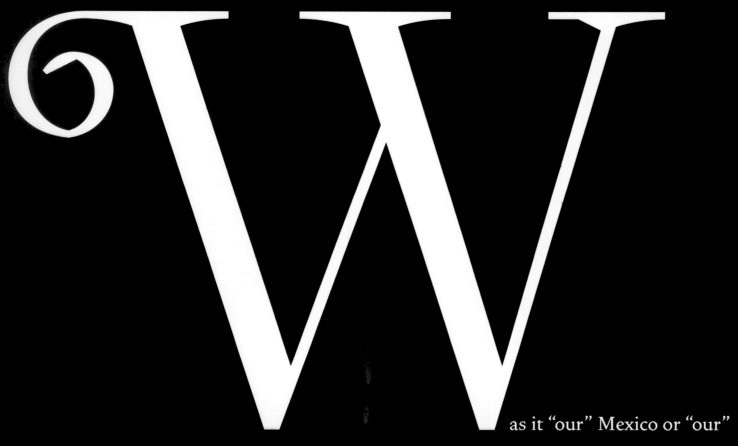

as it "our" Mexico or "our" Italy or "our" Spain in which the well-to-do of booming Los Angeles in the mid-1920s sought to live? It was something of all of these. And if you were firmly middle-class and wanted to live in the foothills above Los Angeles, in a sparely wooded draw or a wide ravine (*cañada*) of the San Gabriel Mountains, in what sort of house should you live? How would your home embody what you went up into those hills to acquire?

That question hangs, not fully resolved, over the figured doorways, bellying archway surrounds, and filigreed grillwork of the Guerra Estate in what is now La Cañada Flintridge at the eastern end of the Crescenta Valley. Built originally for James Degnan in 1927 and designed by Paul Williams, the house combines an assertive "silversmith-style" entry that looks back to sixteenth-century Spain, a ballroom that recalls the villas of Renaissance Italy, and a flight of outdoor steps that have the measured pace of classical antiquity.

Williams, who was justly famous for his adept processing of elements such as these into a "Mediterranean" architecture that was both restrained and lively, never made an ideology of his style, perhaps because, as the first black architect west of the Mississippi, he couldn't afford to. He learned to sketch house plans upside down so that the width of his office desk would separate him from clients who would have been anxious sitting shoulder-to-shoulder with a black man. He designed the houses his clients wanted in whatever architecture they thought would flatter their taste. Perhaps he sketched upside down because he preferred to keep himself a little distant from his clients, too. But he also gave them great style.

The Guerra Estate has recently been restored, and the stairs that descend past the garden now take the visitor down to a guesthouse flooded with light and outfitted with a fine collection of painted Monterey-style furniture, popular from the 1930s through the mid-1940s and itself a synthesis of Arts and Crafts and Spanish colonial forms with decorative

motifs that are Western (by way of Hollywood) and often rendered as whimsical and knowingly primitive. It may be an odd hybrid, but the furniture is both comfortable and lighthearted.

Incongruity is a style, too. The gardens at the Guerra Estate assemble (without any fuss) Moorish tiled fountains, Italian della Robbia ceramic plaques, and faux rustic details that might have come from an eighteenth-century English manor.

Is that what a home in a California canyon should be? The visitor passes the doors of Spain, through the loggias of Italy, under ceilings decorated as if for a banquet hall in Mexico City, across a floor in black-and-white domino as if this were Venice, past geometric tile work from North Africa, and into the light and air of an early California evening. Having crossed so many boundaries of time and space, the house may seem slightly unreal as a consequence.

When the evening shadows have run down the canyon walls and silently pooled in the terraced garden under the old olive tree, the details of the Guerra Estate—so many interlocking puzzle pieces—blur more than a little. Then the question of suitability is laid aside. On the *cañada's* steep flank, daylight has almost topped out; below is lavender and gray.

STRAUSS HOME

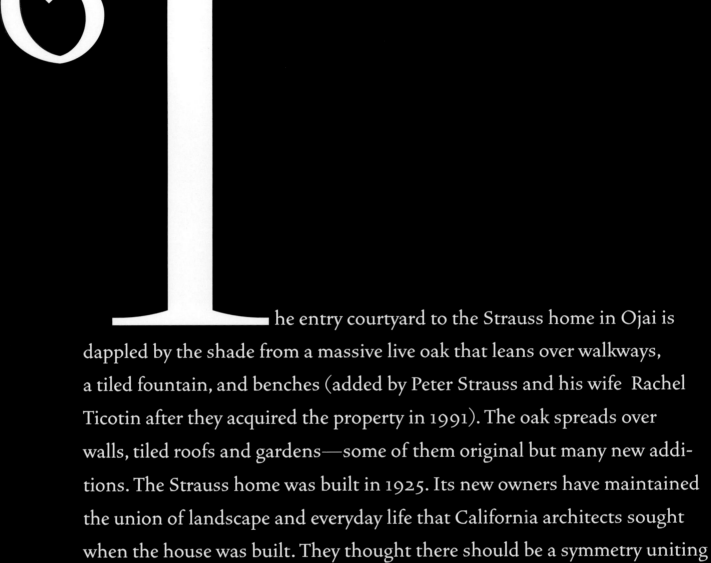

T

he entry courtyard to the Strauss home in Ojai is dappled by the shade from a massive live oak that leans over walkways, a tiled fountain, and benches (added by Peter Strauss and his wife Rachel Ticotin after they acquired the property in 1991). The oak spreads over walls, tiled roofs and gardens—some of them original but many new additions. The Strauss home was built in 1925. Its new owners have maintained the union of landscape and everyday life that California architects sought when the house was built. They thought there should be a symmetry uniting the interior life of the householder, the shape of the house around him, and the sprawling garden that was California beyond his door.

Houses in the Spanish Colonial Revival style only seem to be backward looking to purists. To their architects and their first owners, houses like this one were located in the future, where Californians have always longed to be. The houses are romantic, but they also were anticipatory answers to a modern question: How should Californians live as if they belonged here as much as the oaks and the immemorial curve of sun-browned hills? The Strauss home is an inquiry into this Californian problem and a partial response, just as the town of Ojai was. Ojai's planners and architects

employed motifs from the houses and gardens of Spain, Mexico, Central America, the American Southwest, and North Africa to embody themes of leisure, order, and retreat from a rudely industrializing America.

The light pouring into the patio of this house and its series of room-like gardens is part of that original conception of life in California. Wallace Neff, George Washington Smith, and Lillian Rice among other architects nurtured a utopian aspiration—that the imagination would be illuminated by the Californian sunlight and the enlightened imagination would build a better home for Californians. After all, every house is a pattern for imagining how to live. In the spare whiteness of its stuccoed walls, in the intricate geometry of its glazed tiles, and in its many repetitions of simple design elements, this house reveals that larger purpose. It shows how space might be domesticated. "Paradoxically," as architect and historian Witold Rybczynski has noted, such domesticity "depend(s) on the development of a rich interior awareness."

Architects in the Californian tradition at the turn of the twentieth century wanted to house imaginations in very specific ways. Patterns in structure, in light, and in the rows of an orange grove are more than formal design. The 30-plus acres of valencia and navel orange trees on the grounds of the Strauss home aren't decorative (they produce almost 500 tons of a commercial crop a year) but they are extraordinarily beautiful . . . and an assertion that the qualities of beauty and utility are compatible, almost synonymous.

In the simple rooms of his house and in its gardens—cactus, herb, shade, and Mediterranean among them—Peter Strauss (actor and dedicated gardener) finds the space to let his imagination grow.

GRAVES
HOUSE

alifornia craftsmen, Native American weavers,
and Mexican American potters in the 1920s furnished the grand homes
of the Spanish Colonial Revival with furniture and decorations in imitation
of antique originals, but the sources could be exotic, too—Tunisian tile
makers, Persian metalsmiths, and even cash-strapped Spanish ex-grandees.
It was common for well-to-do owners to assemble at least some of their
home's furnishings, bringing back from European holidays new objects
of their desire (often chosen with the urging of interior decorators who
traveled with them). Their casual eclecticism never pretended historical
authenticity, only a love of novelty that seemed in character with the houses.
Eras, empires, and continents mixed informally in rooms washed in genuine
California sunlight. A Native American shawl draped over a seventeenth-
century Italian refectory table set with Talavera pottery from Mexico under

126

an Ottoman lantern fabricated in Pasadena is the image that many *House Beautiful* layouts perpetuated. Sometimes the result could be severe and churchly, as if the room were waiting for a Spanish bishop to arrive. At their best, the rooms offered relaxation and distraction from the worlds of business and moneyed society.

The playfulness in the Spanish Colonial Revival style—and its popularity—led some manufacturers to market lines of furniture that imitated the better imitations of Spanish, Italian, and Moorish designs in the homes of the wealthy. Barker Brothers—a leading Los Angeles home furnishings retailer—turned to the Mason Furniture Company in 1929 to turn out a 24-piece line of affordable furniture with Spanish themes called Monterey (after the former provincial capital of Alta California). The name was apt, because Monterey was itself a hybrid place, half New England and half Old Mexico. An architecture that blended American and indigenous traditions made an impression on the architects of the Spanish Colonial Revival, but Barker Brothers, in amalgamating the Old West and Old Mexico, was aiming at a different market, one that wanted novelty but nothing too removed from the reassuring comforts of familiar American things. The couch and easy chair might be upholstered in a fabric vaguely like a poncho, but the frame is a simple recycled Craftsman design and available in shades of Old Red, Spanish Blue, Desert Dust, and Straw Ivory.

The mix was a hit. Colorful, unpretentious, and middle class, the Monterey style could be applied to every room in the house and to every convenience, from floor lamps to radio cabinets, and on everything from baby cribs to pianos. Craftsman and Spanish Revival decorative elements recycled through the tile work and painted surfaces, but often the motifs were rough caricatures of the West—serape draped sleeping Mexicans, dashing *vaqueros* on horseback, or blooming saguaro cactus.

The best Monterey pieces, including those Maxine Graves and her late husband collected, have a lightheartedness that accepts that we're all in on the joke. The table and chairs may be reminiscent of rancho originals, but the carving, wood burning, stenciling and wrought-iron hardware happily assert that the pieces were made for the pleasure of owning something entirely new (but that looked curiously old).

Many of the pieces in the Graves collection were factory painted by local craftsman Juan Intenoche. His tableaux of Mexican peasants and grizzled *caballeros* are Anglo fantasies of life south-of-the-border. But his flowers—often abstractions of *rosas de Castilla* (the roses of the Virgin of Guadalupe) —bloom and wreathe on every flat surface, including both the case and bench of the rare Monterey style piano done in "Spanish Green."

The style evolved though the 1930s into the cowboy-obsessed 1940s, but didn't linger long after the start of World War II. Juan Intenoche went to work for Disney.

The eclipse of a style starts a harsh triage of everything the style touched. Junked, forgotten, handed down, left for the thrift shop or the breakers of storage lockers (who buy, almost sight unseen, the units on which the rent is in arrears), the much handled things of someone's everyday life passes through the furnace of circumstance. The Graves rescued their remarkable collection, much of it from swap meets. Oddly, they accomplished for the mass produced objects of a department store the same resurrection the decorators and architects of the grand houses of the Spanish Colonial Revival performed on the debris of Spanish cultural history after World War I.

RANCHO

DE LOS

QUIOTES

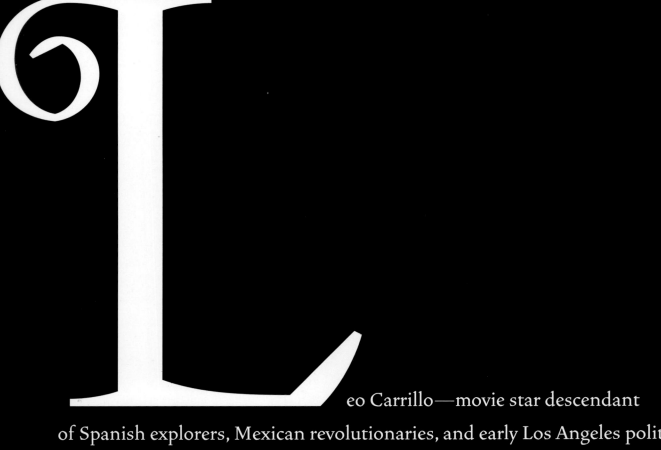

Leo Carrillo—movie star descendant
of Spanish explorers, Mexican revolutionaries, and early Los Angeles politi-
cians—assembled 2,538 acres of gently folded rangeland on the California
coast near Carlsbad and built, between 1937 and his death in 1961, a modern
rancho where dreams of California worked. That they worked reflects the
man, who had been a journeyman actor in every form of show business
since 1913: in vaudeville, on Broadway, in the movies, and, at end, on 1950s
television. That his house and ranch buildings still dream, long after, in the
dense golden light of an autumn afternoon, embodies Carrillo's intense
longing for a part of California that was just beyond his grasp.

      Carrillo had grown up in a storied landscape, shaped by accounts
of California's colonial-era *hidalgos* who also were his great-grandparents.
That landscape, all the more romantic because Carrillo, as a young man in
the 1890s, had seen it pass into other hands, could still be imaginatively
restored, he believed. The houses he built, first in Santa Monica (*Los Alisos*)
and later the *Ranchomich de los Quiotes* (the name refers to the "Spanish
Dagger" agaves that crowded the slopes among the folds of the hills), were

deliberately anachronistic: adobe walls, boulders from the bed of nearby arroyos, axe-cut beams, and plank doors bound with handmade ironwork. Pretend nostalgia applied these elements to finer, architect-built homes between 1900 and 1940, but at least Carrillo's longing for a lost place of romance had been bred into him.

The low, U-shaped main house of the *Rancho de los Quiotes*, made up of three structures joined by tiled roofs, remembers the early Santa Monica home of Andrés Machado, Carrillo's great-uncle. But much of the rest of the house—and other buildings on the rancho grounds—are subtly oriented to other memories. The pair of tall, corner fireplaces at each end of the main room are more New Mexican than Californian, reflecting the background of the Mendoza family members who built the house and who carried out in their carpentry and stonework the rhythms of New Mexico's different building traditions. Although Cliff May, the talented builder of suburban ranch-style houses, is said to have had a hand in the design of *Rancho de los Quiotes*, the house is more plainly a mixture of Carrillo's and the Mendozas' companionable memories of home.

Today the rancho is a national historic landmark and a twenty-seven-acre Carlsbad city park with a lively schedule of tours and public programs. It welcomes today, as it did when Carrillo's Hollywood friends gathered, a little stiffly it seems in photographs, in its unpretentious rooms and on a courtyard patio banked with flowers and guarded by the hooks and spines of cactus and yucca.

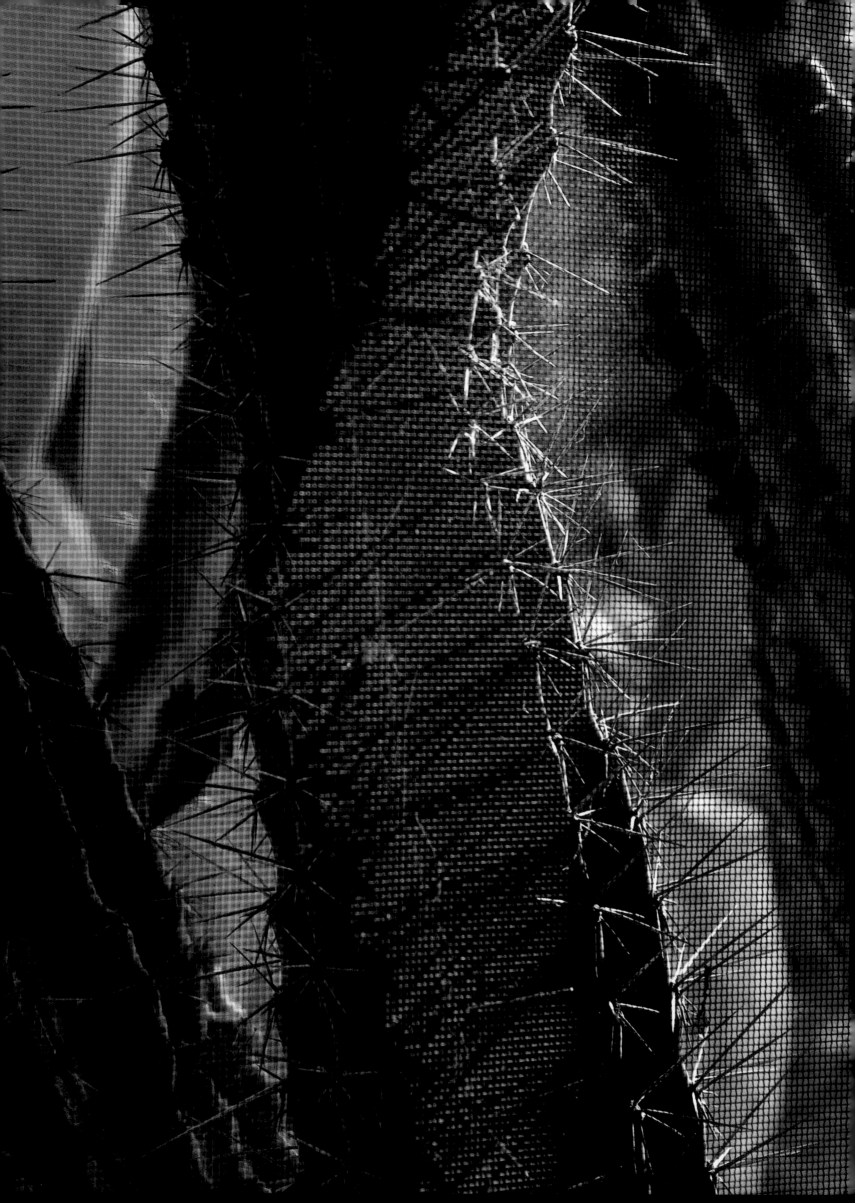

The *Rancho de los Quiotes* is an imaginative projection of the past in the form of a house, but it is not a re-creation. The style is always *mestizo* in inspiration: a mix-up of distant Spain, present Mexico, something of Hollywood, something indigenous to the carpenters who built it, and some things so elemental that they have only simple names. The fired tiles of the roof undulate in the same arc over and over, but the repetition is broken off, askew, handmade, timeworn, poised between then and now. The chipped whitewash reveals as much as it covers up. The light falling on rusted iron hardware and across rough stonework does nothing more than make particular what otherwise would be commonplace. The obvious touch of hands in the plaster molding around door and window openings is a mark made in time, wanting to last.

The Carrillo house isn't only in the landscape. *Rancho de los Quiotes* is literally made of the land. Wide adobe bricks (formed of mud and straw, three at a time in a wood frame) furnished the walls of the main house and patio, the arcade's arches, and the barn and bunkhouse. Carrillo had deliberately sought out places where adobe would surround him, as it had in the stories he had been told in which dashing men on horseback and women in silk shawls embroidered in Manila moved as if in a dream. In *The California I Love*, his autobiography, Carrillo addressed his readers, "Now, amigos, perhaps you understand why the adobe is my birthstone."

VILLA
AURORA

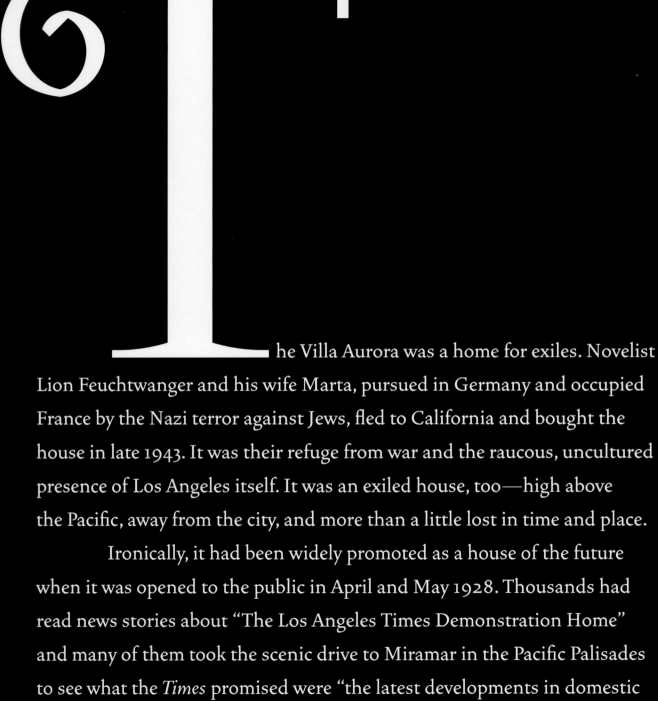

The Villa Aurora was a home for exiles. Novelist Lion Feuchtwanger and his wife Marta, pursued in Germany and occupied France by the Nazi terror against Jews, fled to California and bought the house in late 1943. It was their refuge from war and the raucous, uncultured presence of Los Angeles itself. It was an exiled house, too—high above the Pacific, away from the city, and more than a little lost in time and place.

Ironically, it had been widely promoted as a house of the future when it was opened to the public in April and May 1928. Thousands had read news stories about "The Los Angeles Times Demonstration Home" and many of them took the scenic drive to Miramar in the Pacific Palisades to see what the *Times* promised were "the latest developments in domestic technology and home planning." In fact, it was a sales gimmick to lure

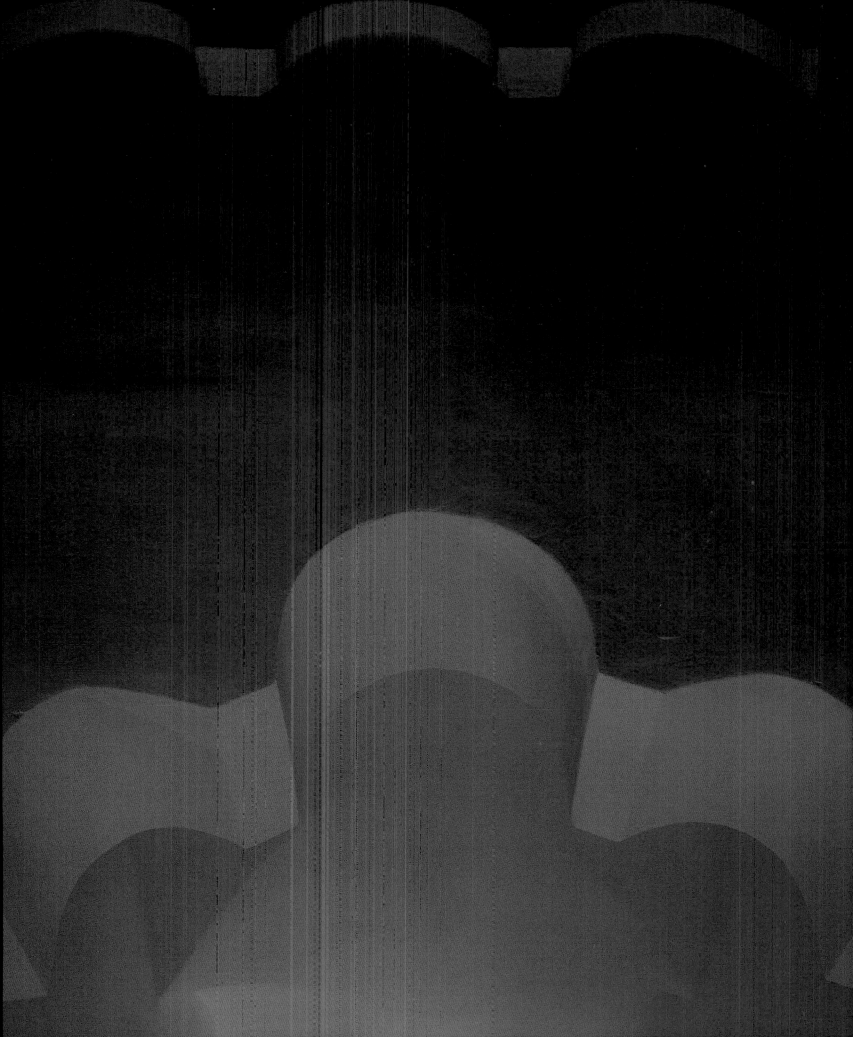

prospective buyers into the distant Santa Monica foothills, but the house did include a kitchen with laborsaving appliances (including an electric dishwasher) and other up-to-date amenities. That the house was designed in a period style did not seem incongruous with its all-electric modernity. The Demonstration Home did not enclose real history; it was thoroughly new.

That may help explain why the expatriate Feuchtwangers were attracted to it. The house had the dreamy presence, some had said, of a castle in Spain, but the well-traveled Feuchtwangers knew how false that was. It was a place without a past, and the Feuchtwangers welcomed into it other exiles escaping brutal memories and dreading places from which they might have to flee again. They were German émigrés mostly: Bertolt Brecht, Kurt Weill, Heinrich and Thomas Mann, Arnold and Gertrude Schoenberg, and Franz Werfel among them.

That bitter period is commemorated by the house today. Operating as a non-profit foundation funded in part by the German government, the house provides residencies to young writers and artists from Germany. There is a yearly program of public events and lectures. The foundation also awards a residency to a persecuted writer or one forced into exile.

Now called the Villa Aurora (and sensitively reconstructed in 1996 under the direction of Los Angeles architect Frank Dimster), the house—with its 14 rooms on three floors—is distinguished by a profusion of wainscoting, plaques, and "carpets" of majolica tile produced by the Hispano-Moresque Company of Los Angeles. The intricate counterpoint

of the tile work is suspended on backdrops of white stucco, round and elliptical arches, sawtooth brackets, and stout piers and pillars. The architectural effects are loosely based on the Roman, Moorish, and Middle Eastern elements fused in a style called Mudéjar (the name refers to the followers of Islam who continued to practice the old religion after the reconquest of Spain by Christian Aragon and Castile in 1492). An early twentieth century revival later splashed its brightly patterned surfaces on the buildings of Seville's Ibero-American Exposition of 1929.

As retranslated by architect Mark Daniels (with interior details and ceiling designs by the painter Thorwald Probst), the exuberance of Mudéjar was modulated for more temperate Los Angeles homebuyers. Bight tile contrasts with broad stretches of white stucco under a typical pantile roof. The sober living room, with its hooded fireplace and scant decorative elements, opens to a loggia. A painted ceiling traces arabesques. A courtyard offers silence and walled security. Balconies and arcades look seaward above the tumbled wall of an arroyo.

The Villa Aurora clings to its slice of suburban hillside and gazes at the horizon. To the Feuchtwangers, who would never return to the Germany that rejected them, the house must have seemed beautiful and placeless, as so much of California seemed to its many waves of expatriates, émigrés, and unsettled wanderers. California, too, is a home for exiles.

DOLGEN HOUSE

In a seemingly empty place—empty of familiar associations, of the much handled things of one's youth, above all, empty of memories—new Californians yearned to build. At the start of the twentieth century, even before the hammering together of pioneer shelter was over, wealthy Californians (nearly all of them recent immigrants from the East or Midwest) sought to fill the emptiness of California with something that would satisfy their longing for home. Richard Requa, like other architects in the Arts and Crafts tradition, believed that satisfying such longings required an amalgam of romance, the "spirit of place," the picturesque, and the nobly domestic, all of which was epitomized on the grandest of scales in the buildings and grounds of the 1915 Panama-California Exposition in San Diego.

The exposition defined a new building style and gave it a name: Spanish Revival. Requa, as did other architects associated with the exposition, made plausible claims about climate, landscape, and history to

stitch San Diego to likely places in Spain, the Southern France, Italy, North Africa, and even Persia. But the Spanish Revival wasn't really a revival of anything, since nothing like this architecture had ever existed in colonial California. Requa rightly called his synthesis "Southern California Architecture" and left it at that.

(Requa made extended trips to Central America and Cuba and in 1926 and 1928 to North Africa and southern Europe. These travels were sponsored by Monolith Portland Cement, whose products were perfect for recreating, with American durability, the forms of Mediterranean architecture. Less able builders quickly reimagined Requa's eclecticism in thousands of almost-*casitas* on miles of suburban streets.)

The Dolgen House on Coronado Island, built in 1926, expresses some of the boundaries of Requa's Southern California style. The horseshoe arches and the pierced sheetwork lamps recall Morocco or Tunisia. The parabolic arches that open from the entry are North African in inspiration. Shouldered flat arches and elongated elliptical arches, characteristic of Mediterranean building traditions, frame windows and doorways. The massive fireplace in the living room would suit a villa or hacienda (except the crown-like lamp under the ribbed belly of the ceiling is not in the same provincial idiom). And the little balcony that projects over the front entry would allow the sequestered women of the household to inspect comings and goings in the street below, if there were a street below and if this were a house in Fez.

In this house and in others, Requa acknowledged the exoticism that delighted his clients even as he subtly circumscribed its effects. The architectural forms are generalized, but that was part of his style, too, influenced by the early Modernism of the San Diego architect Irving Gill for whom Requa worked between 1907 and 1912. The overall impression is deliberately abstract, but then a square of light through a pierced lampshade patterns a stretch of white wall and an entire room seems to concentrate in that detail.

The flat diamonds of the second floor balcony repeat in greater contrast in the grill of the stairway window—another concentrating detail. And there are many others: the inverted steps of the entry brackets (holding up the balcony from whose windows no veiled woman ever watched) repeat the sequence of steps into the house; the joining of three deep arches in a pilaster also opens a gray-and-gold fold in space; and a metal sheathed lamp does not shine, it holds the light in.

Requa was a great collector and popularizer of forms intended to reconcile contradictions: being modern and having a tradition (even if the tradition had to be invented ad hoc). His reconciling Southern California style—with broad sweeps of plastered or stuccoed wall, heavily tiled roofs, wrought iron ornamentation, and odd chimney designs— flowered again, near the end of his career (he died in 1941) in his designs for the California-Pacific International Exhibition of 1935 in San Diego.

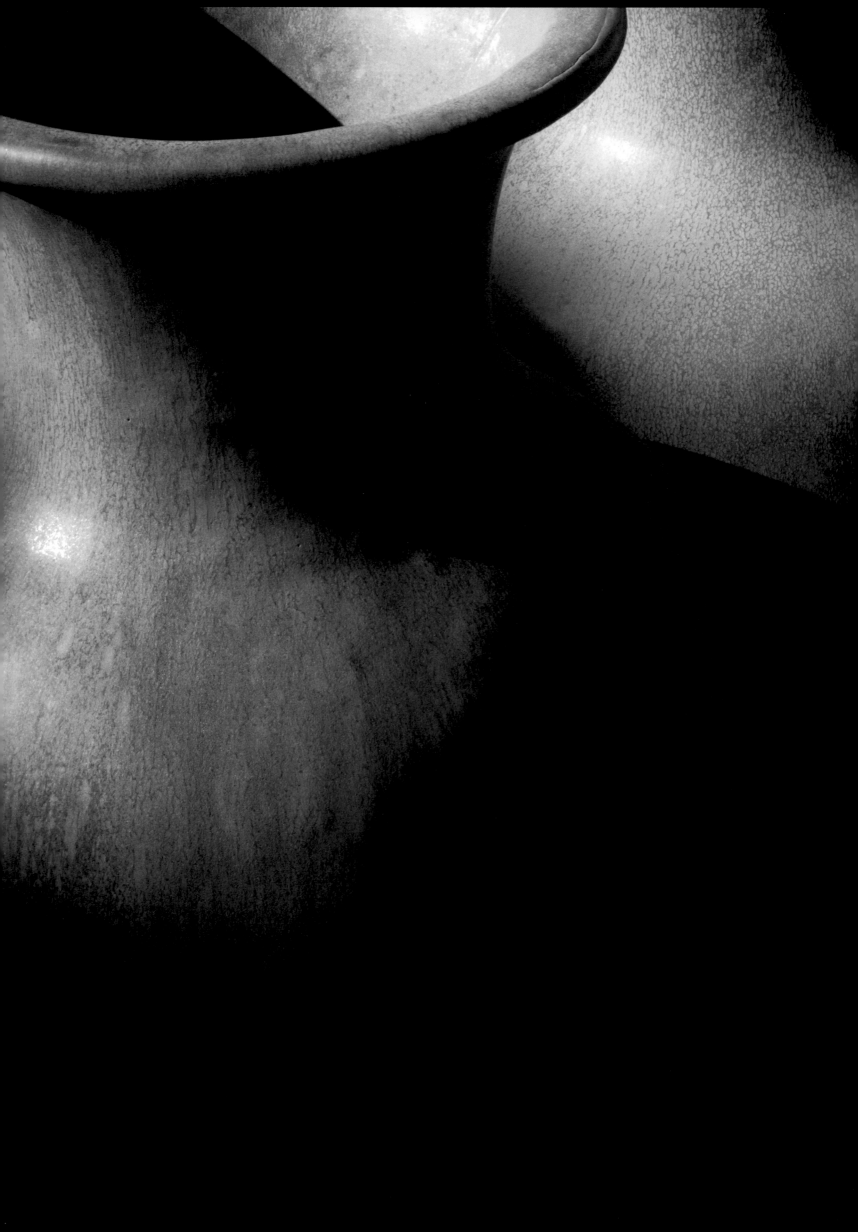

CASA
DEL
HERRERO

In the black-and-white photographs in the May 1926 edition of *Pacific Coast Architect*, *Casa del Herrero* (The Blacksmith's House) stands a little stiffly as an emblem of good taste in the style that was then called Spanish Revival. The plain stuccoed walls, wrought-iron grill-work, wood-framed balconies, and ordered gardens suggest southern Spain—Andalusia, specifically—not the eighteenth- and nineteenth-century rural haciendas of colonial California. The difference was important to architects like George Washington Smith, whose wealthy Midwest clients were anxious that their taste win approval.

The houses of Andalusia and Mexican California share architectural roots—the fortified country villas and simple town houses of medieval Spain—but their imitations in early twentieth-century Santa Barbara and Montecito kept the hierarchies clear. "Old California" was romantic for its half-ruined aspect, but it offered the look of badly maintained mission buildings and shed-like adobes. Spain suggested a kind of domesticated grandeur, if you had the money.

Smith designed *Casa del Herrero* in 1922 for the Steedman family, whose social aspirations matched their comfortable circumstances. George Steedman had made money in Saint Louis during World War I producing machinery and munitions. Santa Barbara beckoned in the 1920s, as it did for many, as a place of ease in the winter sunshine where middle-class Midwesterners were easily welcomed into society. Steedman also was a collector, a talented metalworker, and a patron of architecture. Smith and Steedman are said to have collaborated on the design of the *Casa del Herrero* (punning on the owner's trade and the ironwork Steedman himself forged for the house). Perhaps, after laboring over hundreds of revisions to the design, they just called it a draw.

The result was a plan of casual asymmetries that characteristically, for Smith, blends the house and its grounds into a rhythmic pattern. Pattern moved Smith, who had a fondness for what was simple, boldly drawn, and flattened into a surface. Smith had been a well-regarded Post-Impressionist painter before he took up architecture. He knew the work of Gauguin and Cézanne and witnessed the onset of Cubism in Europe. He had seen the architecture of the early modernists before returning to America in 1914. Although always building in a recognizably historical style, Smith was aware that his designs were new and direct, too, even if they reflected the expectations of his clients and would never be as radical as Schindler's or Neutra's.

The *Casa del Herrero* has been changed only slightly since its completion in 1925. Its eleven acres of house and grounds unfolds as a series of indoor and outdoor spaces modulated by their enclosures. Some are the formal rooms of the house; others are as simple as a hedge or a length of connecting wall pierced by a row of arches. The multiplication of surfaces provides the canvas (underfoot and all around) on which tiles

(some specially made in Tunis) mark out a geometry that easily expands into grids, water channels, and spaces that are partly Spanish and partly North African.

(The gardens were designed by Ralph Stevens and Lockwood De Forest, Jr., noted Santa Barbara landscape architects, and horticulturalist Peter Riedel.)

Tiles lift up stair treads (on even the servants' back stairs). Tiles panel lavatories, run out of doorways onto floors, and encircle the base of the house like the fringe of a shawl. Tiles surround guests sitting on patio chairs cast by Steedman himself. Tiles lead the eye across the bare whiteness of walls, channel water to fountains with their own tiled basins, and finally collect—a little breathless after all this effort—on quiet garden benches. Smith lets tile (and other patterned surfaces) relieve the plainness of plastered and stuccoed masonry. He lets the tiles guide light over surfaces that give the light back, subtly changed.

Casa del Herrero, now on the National Register of Historic Places, has remained in the same family, one of the few great estates of California to be woven into a single family's story. Today it is being preserved by a non-profit educational foundation for the benefit of the Montecito community.

Exactly what is being protected, however, is only now emerging. Smith and his contemporaries understood that the Spanish Revival was an imagined tradition, a synthetic style, that it was as inauthentic as it was appropriate (and damning it for the authoritarian modernists of the next generation of architects). But when does a made-up tradition become traditional, when does it become the proper shape of the places we long to see?

BLACK
RESIDENCE

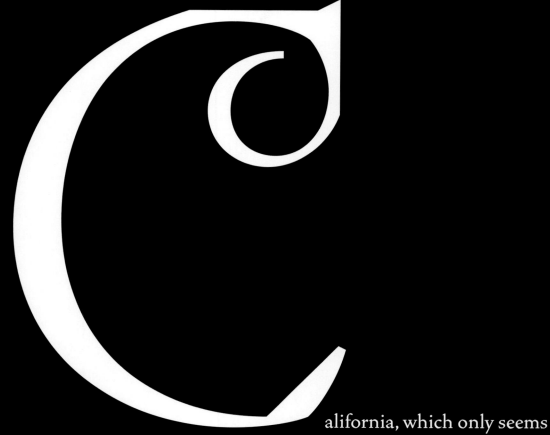

alifornia, which only seems
the chaotic result of the Gold Rush and all the booms in oranges, oil, and
real estate afterwards, actually was carefully planned into existence.
Between 1870 and 1930, frontier California became suburban California,
and the transformation was deliberate and done on an industrial scale.

By 1870, much of the developable land in the southern half of the
state was in the hands of the successors, mostly San Francisco financiers,
of the Mexican colonial-era *haciendados*. Even more of the state—and access
to eastern capital—was in the hands of the big railroads. To sell all this
empty space, the new possessors of the California landscape laid out rural
villages gridded like Midwest farm towns, sold lots in "garden suburbs"
built as models of English town planning, and vigorously marketed
California's most problematic contribution to urban design: the twentieth
century "themed community." Rancho Santa Fe, developed for the

Santa Fe railroad in 1921, shows all the pleasures and contradictions of that beguiling idea.

The railroad brought in development experts—notably Leone G. Sinnard, a civil engineer who drafted the development's overall plan and laid out fifty miles of picturesque winding roads through the San Diego foothills. Afterwards, Sinnard stayed on as the company's chief salesman. The San Diego architectural firm of Requa and Jackson joined the project in 1922, bringing experience with large residential projects. Requa and Jackson also assembled a diverse team of draftsmen and architects to carry out the development theme: thick adobe walls, modest elevations, flat-roofs, and a pallet of exterior colors in shades of ocher, blue, and green. The railroad (already heavily invested in its own mythology of the Southwest) initially wanted to evoke a Navajo pueblo, not a village in Andalusia.

Requa understood the allure of unadorned cubes, arches, and wall surfaces. He had apprenticed with Irving Gill in his San Diego office between 1907 and 1912, when Gill was taking the simple elements of mission and pueblo architecture in the direction of greater abstraction. Requa, even in his fashionable houses of the 1920s, grounded what he called the "Southern California style" in Gill's pure forms. Requa passed some of that sensibility to the architects who apprenticed in his office, including Lillian Rice who oversaw much of the later development of Rancho Santa Fe.

Rice was an original. She was completely Californian in outlook, which to her meant the subordination of structure to landscape. She had been among the first three women to graduate from Berkeley's School of Architecture. As one of Requa's favored designers, Rice was soon turning his finished sketches into buildable plans. And she was only 34 when she became Rancho Santa Fe's resident architect. A school, a library, a cluster of commercial buildings, and residential commissions quickly followed for Rice.

But Rancho Santa Fe changed during those years. The wealthy homeowners who controlled its development abandoned the unsettling mixture of Mexican and Native American motifs in Requa's original concept for the more fashionable Spanish Colonial Revival style. After 1928, the walls of new houses were required to be white and their roofs to be tiled.

Rice was adept at designing for these owners. She built homes that welcomed the embrace of the landscape just beyond low garden walls—houses filled with light and a quality of domesticity that Rice herself claimed was her contribution as a woman architect. She stayed on in Rancho Santa Fe as both an architect and a leading member of the powerful Art Jury that ruled on the design of new homes.

Rice, like other California architects of the 1920s, believed that she was making a new kind of architecture and not merely a transient style. Rancho Santa Fe was meant to realize that large ambition, which was as much California's as hers. "To conform to the setting of nature" was Rice's own formulation of that intersection of architecture and place. Their union in these photographs of the Black Residence is in the pale rose of the stucco, the rectangle of the entry facade, the upward flight of tiles on the stairs, and the tactile appeal of every surface.

The Rancho Santa Fe homeowners association, with Rice's strong encouragement, embodied California's aspirations for art and nature in the contractual details of property ownership. As a result of deed restrictions that still constrain this "themed community," there is a kind of timelessness there, among the eucalyptus groves the Santa Fe railroad had planted in the mistaken belief they would provide cheap lumber for railroad ties. And that bit of industrial history is part of the contradiction of Rancho Santa Fe, too. Among trees planted as industrial raw material, beautiful homes reach out to a landscape carefully constructed to be "all of nature."

WILK-BURCH HOUSE

rchitects Diane Wilk
and Michael Burch were looking for a house from California's Spanish
Colonial Revival, a period that has the intense pull of memory for Michael
Burch, who had grown up in Pasadena. They found a home—a little dishev-
eled—built by the popular southern Californian architect Arthur Kelly
for his own family in a foothill development then called Alta Canyada (now
La Cañada-Flintridge). The Kelly Residence, as described in the May 22,
1925, edition of *Southwest Builder and Contractor*, was of frame and stucco
construction with a tile roof, hardwood floors, decorated beams, ornamental
ironwork, an "art stone" fireplace mantel, and fixtures and appliances
that a modern home required. Kelly's 2,300-square-foot house cost $12,000
to build, making it fairly typical of the upper-middle class Spanish-style
houses of Los Angeles in the 1920s.

Kelly's architectural practice was busy and eclectic. He had begun
his career working for the Greene brothers in Pasadena. When he opened
his own architectural office in 1907, he designed homes in the still popular
Craftsman style. In the 1920s, in partnership with Joseph Estep, he designed residences for clients in Beverly Hills, Holmby Hills, and San Marino.

Most of these commissions were Spanish Colonial Revival in inspiration (including the ranch house built for cowboy actor William S. Hart in Newhall). But many of Kelly's commissions were in the Tudor Revival style; one of these is now the Playboy mansion.

The Alta Canyada home passed through the hands of several owners after Kelly gave up the property in 1938. Wilk and Burch bought it in 1999 and with great sensitivity, completed a restoration of the house and gardens. They discovered, when they became the parents of triplets, that they really needed more of a house. Their additions—for children, a family room/media room, a contemporary kitchen, master suite bathrooms, and office space for both architects—were neither preservation nor reinterpretation. "I am interested in something that is 'timeless' because it is traditional," notes Michael Burch. "The vocabulary of the Spanish Colonial Revival is already so expansive that it is almost unlimited in the possibilities that can be done with it. The style is a natural fit for Californians, culturally, historically, and climatically. And it is romantic, but in the non-pejorative sense of freedom from the strictures of classicism. It is serenity, plasticity, and simplicity. It is the lack of pretentiousness."

From the street, the Wilk-Burch home is a single story, centered on an entry in the form of a tall drum and pointed arch that echo a form Wallace Neff popularized. From the street level, the house descends the hillside to what had been the maid's quarters and garage beneath the house. The descent is managed by a sequence of stairs that unfolds from entry hall

through a horseshoe arch, and along a lavishly tiled hallway. "There is light at every axis," the architect/owners point out, making movement a compelling orientation toward California sunshine. That light, by design, moves through and over all the spaces of the house and its grounds, guiding and shaping. Light and shadow have largely replaced ornament.

Where the workman's art is revealed it is often in the form of imperfection. For Wilk and Burch, "The human hand is apparent in just about all the materials of the house, from the roughness of the stone pavers, the texture of the plaster on the walls, and the unevenness of the paint colors. The detail in the carving of the beams in the living room ceiling, the carving on all the cabinet doors, the stenciling with its brush strokes—all show the human hand."

"Why do we love the Spanish style?" they ask. "It goes back to a sense of mystery and the serenity and calmness that come out of simplicity and the use of materials of the earth and the human hand in their production. The style responds to our emotional needs. Spanish style houses are serene, rooted to their surroundings, and their heritage."

Rooted in time and place and in an idea of California that welcomed the picturesque and the playful, the Wilk-Burch House remains, even as it has adapted to twenty-first century needs, essentially romantic. "It is romantic," Diane Wilk and Michael Burch emphasize, "because of the light in the evening and the golden glow of light at daybreak, and the unexpected play of shadows throughout the day."

HOFER
HOUSE

Brett Hofer no longer lives in the Laguna Beach house that took two decades to evolve from a standard "dwelling unit"— a stucco box for living—into a contemporary reimagining of what the Spanish style had meant and what it can mean still. The Hofer House is a poetic image of the past, just as the houses of the Spanish Colonial Revival were, but it also engages in a complex dialog with what it means to be new (and that complexity also was part of the revivalist project at the turn of the twentieth century).

Hofer drew his image of home from boyhood visits to his grand-mother's Spanish style house and from the austere presence of Southern California's Franciscan missions and the hybrid Mission-style architecture

they briefly influenced. This revivalist lineage ran parallel in California architecture with the native abstraction of Irving Gill in the 1910s and the International Modernism of Richard Neutra and Rudolf Schindler in the 1920s. What connected Spanish revivalists, the idiosyncratic Gill, and triumphant modernists? It was all the possibilities of California at a time when everything in California—even nostalgia—was new.

Hofer is an artist not an architect, and just as George Washington Smith did in 1918, he designed his home from memory and example and with an imagination roomy enough for both the traditional and the modern. Smith saw Andalusian farmsteads as rooted in a specific past and as abstract forms for sheltering a new way of life. Hofer saw the persistence of those sheltering forms in the landscape of his childhood and read back into them their connection to a life in California. The design of his house, different from Smith's in result but not in spirit, aptly combines what is modest, direct, and undogmatic in California architecture, as if the authorities of twentieth-century modernity had never lost their memories. "Modern antiquity" is Hofer's name for this mixture of influences (which include his collection of notably plain Monterey-style furniture and other decorative elements). "I kept to a theme, but I kept it ambiguous," Hofer notes, and perhaps his embrace of that in-between state is another reflection on what it means to be romantic.

The romantic intuition of the Hofer House is its Gill-inspired simplicity. It links the geometry of the series of elongated arches framing the entry, the monastic composure of a sleeping niche and its unadorned bed, and the high modernist rectangle of the studio/office (whose glass enclosure reframes the perennial Californian desire to mingle landscape and living space). Simplicity, as Gill understood it, was never unimaginative; what was removed always revealed.

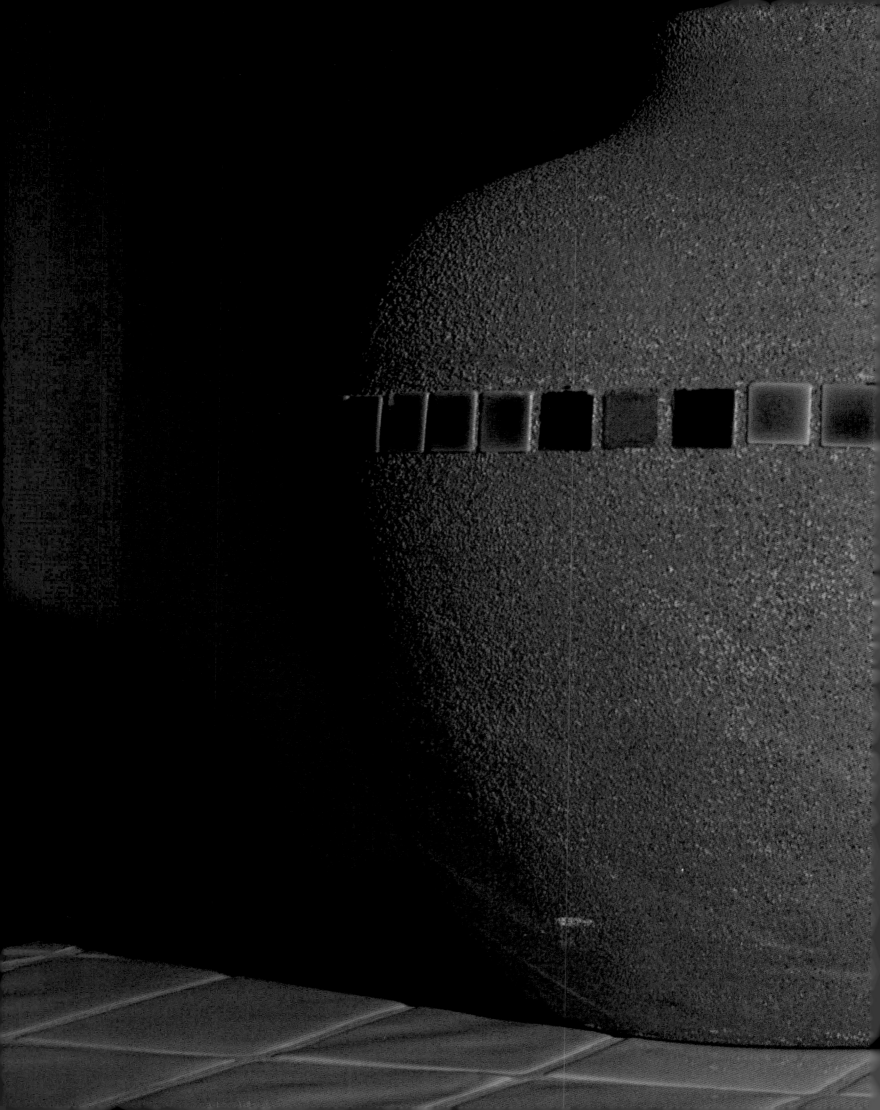

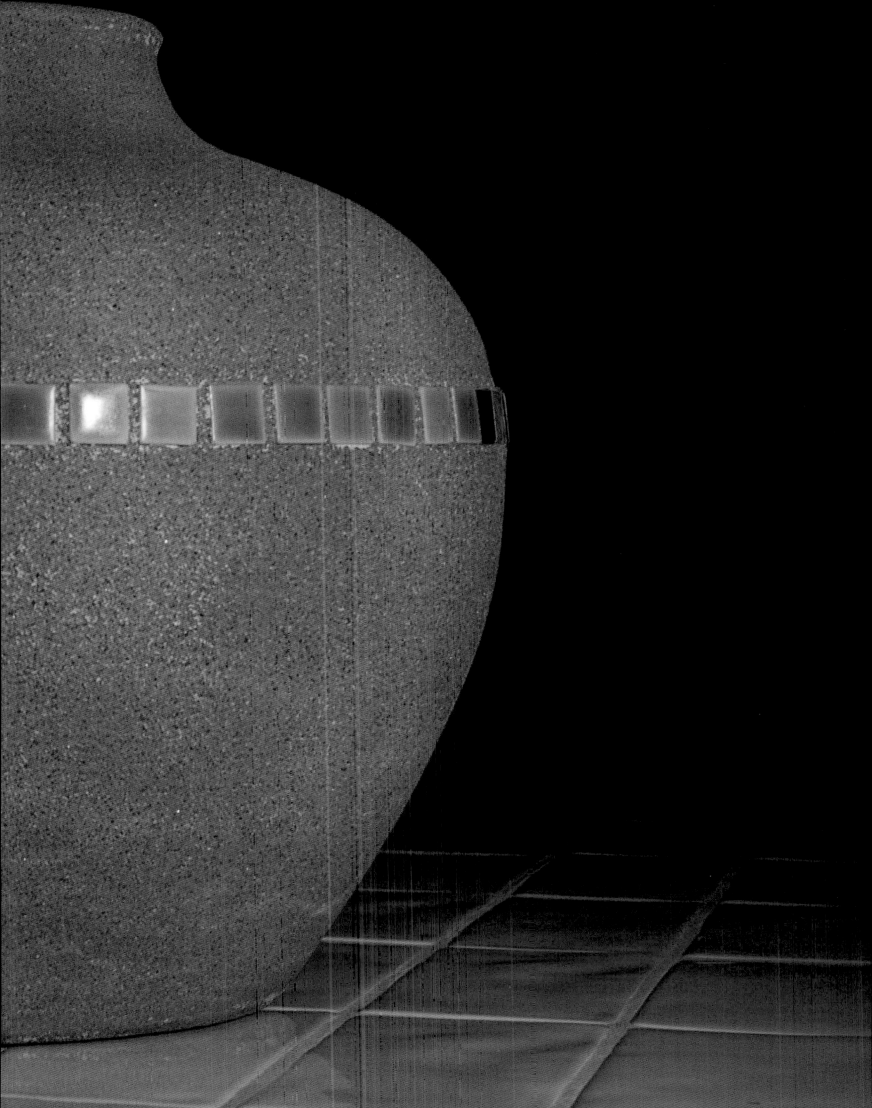

Simplicity also characterizes the collection of concrete jars and vases—originally intended for outdoor use—that Hofer assembled. The concrete is unexpectedly light (the forms were spun into shape, Hofer points out, not cast), and nearly all of the containers are decorated with colored tiles—square, hexagonal, or mosaic—in a band around the widest part. You can see the grain in the surface and the irregularities in the hand placement of the tiles. You are reminded that honest concrete was Gill's favored material, just as it was Le Corbusier's.

These containers, equally ordinary and monumental, replay the themes of the Hofer House: what is new inevitably becomes a tradition; what is outside will not be kept at bay but can be made a houseguest; forms have functions but they also have a inner life of their own apart from their use and apart from us.

All houses are haunted, even the most modern and pitiless ones, by all the houses before it. Houses haunt themselves even, by evoking a memory, allowing shadows, or wearing a pattern on a perfectly smooth white wall. Brett Hofer agrees his house has that quality; he deliberately sought it, he says. Like the grand houses in the Spanish Colonial Revival style, his house allows admixture, continuity, and the presence of what has come before.

CASA ROMANTICA

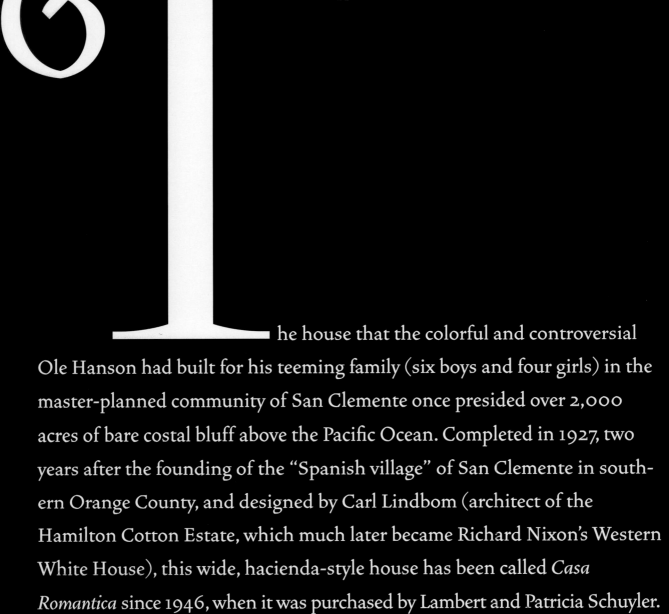

he house that the colorful and controversial Ole Hanson had built for his teeming family (six boys and four girls) in the master-planned community of San Clemente once presided over 2,000 acres of bare costal bluff above the Pacific Ocean. Completed in 1927, two years after the founding of the "Spanish village" of San Clemente in southern Orange County, and designed by Carl Lindbom (architect of the Hamilton Cotton Estate, which much later became Richard Nixon's Western White House), this wide, hacienda-style house has been called *Casa Romantica* since 1946, when it was purchased by Lambert and Patricia Schuyler.

Ole Hanson did not have many years as a make-believe *haciendado* in his equally make-believe Spanish village as, for too many sellers of dreams in California, reality crashed in after 1929. Even while the Depression deepened, even after Orange County boomed again, the essentials of San

Clemente remained: a white sketch of walls outlined by red tile roofs above blue water.

The house today is a community center with tours, school programs, and a nationally known literary reading series.

Casa Romantica served its first owners as a template for the kind of life to which they aspired. (For Hanson, it also was a sales pitch to the kind of well-to-do buyers he sought for the acres of house lots he hoped to sell as quickly as possible). For us, walking the house's surround of tiled arcades, crossing its spacious patios, and standing in its columned, over-sized rooms, *Casa Romantica* is, even more, a way of seeing.

It is a way of seeing how big, simple shapes are regularly repeated in columns, balustrades, archways, doorways, and the intersections of the interior spaces these forms enclose. These simple patterns reference a kind of elevated provincialism—"our" Spain as seen by talented architects who knew all the classical orders and who could have as easily designed Hanson a Tudor country house or a French chateau with the details almost exactly right. But Hanson and many of his striving contemporaries, eager to reinvent themselves, saw the California coast as a place for which another architecture was wanted. It would not be tied to a past that others had acquired with their wealth. It would be a relatively simple architecture that might also be something beautiful.

The son of Norwegian immigrants born in a cabin outside of Racine, Wisconsin, in 1874, the grown-up Hanson acquired a house of shadows

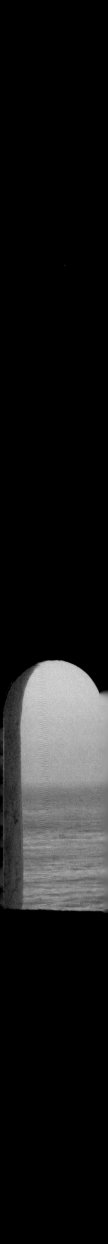

and white walls, of Moorish doorways opening into rooms suitable for a minor grandee, of balconies that offer unlimited vistas west into sunsets and darkening surf.

It is a house that opens into outdoor spaces that enclose like rooms, rooms that open into deeper interiors with the sobriety of a convent, and interiors that then open to the scrub of the plain bluff and the beach and the water. Nearly everything is seen twice: through a door or an archway to another archway just like it or to a door opposite. It is as if the house were presenting a series of propositions about continuity and difference, like the variations on a simple theme in a concerto. Where repeating Roman arches span the perimeter of the room, there is a fountain and a sunken, shallow floor. In this space, a cool, even light moves through the day, marking time more elementally and elegantly than the owner might have ever imagined. A fountain, shade, and cool rooms beyond.

OGILVY
ESTATE

T

he past is an ambiguous guide in the houses in the Spanish Revival style. Does the arrow of time point back to the eighteenth century in Mexico or the seventeenth century in Spain or further back to the eleventh century in Damascus? Surprisingly, the originators of the style said that the arrow pointed toward the future, toward a cosmopolitan architecture made for California, freed from the rigidity of East Coast models, that would take from Mediterranean traditions and blend what was splendid and sheltering in them. And now, many years later, when Modernism itself is just another historical style, what of the passage of time within the houses they built to embody their hope for a new kind of home for a new kind of life?

The home of Mr. and Mrs. Arthur Ogilvy in Montecito, built around 1926, began as a relatively simple design by George Washington Smith with a plan that looked back to the tradition of adobe rectangles that comes from the Mexican period in California (for example, *Rancho de*

los Quiotes on page 142). Originally, the Ogilvy House was a simple H-shape of rooms entered through a tiled hall (enlarging on the covered passage that would have divided the rectangular blocks of rooms of a colonial-era home). The two wings of the house (with bedrooms in one and kitchen and service areas in the other) were joined by a living room and the dining room. Today, these rooms still open, in the fashion preferred by Smith, through French doors to a covered terrace that extend a vista outward to a patio, a fountain, and the garden beyond. A "River of Paradise" tiled in white and blue runs through the garden from a shallow, octagonal pool (a metaphor for source of Eden's rivers, called a *havuz* in Turkish).

Much has changed, however. While some of Smith's basic plan remains—two low arms embracing a wide entry courtyard—the house has been reshaped by other hands.

Patricia Gebhard (in *George Washington Smith: Architect of the Spanish Colonial Revival*, based on her late husband's research) notes that the Ogilvy House was greatly enlarged by its later owners. A tower, second floor, and a staircase that ascends from the dining room were added. The staircase reflects the design of the stairs in the *Casa del Herrero* (page 190), with tiled risers, a wrought iron balustrade, and the same sweeping upward curve.

The Andalusian farmhouses and colonial Mexican haciendas from which Smith drew inspiration, he acknowledged, were not architecture, strictly speaking, but the accretions of time. Smith believed that contemporary architects should emulate the effects of time's slow passage in the design of modern houses and that Californians could live in them as if their houses had been handed down through generations.

Time has passed, even if it is only eighty years, and the architectural rhythms of the Ogilvy House still reveal Smith's concern for textures in smoothed plaster and glowing terracotta. Despite the many changes,

much of Smith's dignified simplicity persists (he was an admirer of
Le Corbusier).

The long corridor through the center of the house still has its monastic qualities: plain and reticent. The light from the garden at the
corridor's end still carries the imagination outward (just as Smith intended). The pale blue, gray, and rust-colored light still falls generously into
rooms that he designed. The movement of shadows over rough stucco,
glazed tile, and painted wood follows cycles that cannot change, even if the
house has been greatly reshaped. What has been added and taken away
by other hands is only the handling that every house endures (and some not
as successfully as this one).

Smith understood that houses are in time and that every house
acquires its own way of being. Smith took the best of his style, he said, from
looking at the traditional houses of Mexico, Spain, Italy, and the south of
France. They were houses through which time has passed slowly enough not
to bear away too much.

EL
BOSQUE

H

ouses in the Spanish Colonial Revival style—beguilingly romantic to the those who commissioned them in the 1920s—seem so necessary now, eighty years after the style flowered and then passed into something far less than a style, more a shorthand of pale stucco and red tile applied to suburban tract houses. What adds to the intensity of our longing is the realization that something was so expertly done, but only briefly at the level of accomplishment seen in the home of Joan and Roger Kreiss in Montecito. Yet if we think that their house recalls only a vanished California of sunshine and ease, we miss the point its architect labored to make.

The home called *El Bosque* was designed by George Washington Smith in 1925 for San Francisco socialite Cecily Casserly. *El Bosque* might be

described as a hope that has the shape of a house. Within its specific architectural properties—light, volume, mass, and texture—is a hope about California. The house had been an anticipatory story about what Californians expected their place to be. For Smith, the story had something to do with pleasure.

It is, first, the pleasure of touch. *El Bosque* comes near the end of the Craftsman tradition in California building, celebrated at the start of the century in the houses designed by the Greene brothers in Pasadena. In *El Bosque*, the Greene's lapidary craftsmanship has been abstracted. Surfaces are not intricately fitted; they are molded, smoothed, rounded, and weighed. In other words, they are handled. And the worker's long-ago touch—sometimes suggested only by a slight roughness—evokes a corresponding sensation of being touched.

Pleasure is movement, too—the eye moving over patterns in tile, patterns in light, and patterns in the grain of wood and wrought iron. Patterns play over a background of arch, bracket, wall, and facade always animating these simple elements, often deepening their relative flatness in the persistent southern Californian sunlight with wedges of shadow. Movement is more than a surface pleasure, however. Within the remarkable interior space of the entryway, for example—at the conjunction of its pointed arches, the formal staircase, and row of treads and risers spiraling up Escher-like overhead—motion seems built into *El Bosque's* revelation of itself. This is pleasure in play.

Yet the house remains inward and familiar, characteristic features of Smith's subtle design philosophy, as well as simple, quiet, and harmonious when its inner life is revealed. The Kreisses discovered that the awkward arrangement of some previously remodeled rooms were resolved when they were returned to the proportions Smith had laid out in his original plan.

Never static, Smith's designs always incorporated asymmetries in the treatment of windows, grills, stairs, and doorways. What could otherwise be blandly monumental acquires a lighter touch, pleasingly balanced by being ever so slightly out of balance. Noting the sweep of a wall that serves to conceal a service entrance, Joan Kreiss points out that in curving the wall, instead of making it a right angle, Smith gave the house a more romantic feel.

To be delighted by the play of architectural elements was the ideal of California architects who, like George Washington Smith, had mastered the knowing historicism and casual modernity in the Spanish Colonial Revival style. Their houses figured in a larger narrative of California that centered on the pleasures Californians expected to find in their adopted state. The sense of poignancy felt today in the work of George Washington Smith is a measure of how much of that story we've misplaced.

The hope of many Californians—then and now—was to be at home in a place in which light and air and landscape merged, a place in which of all of nature and art might be bounded by low garden wall.

ISLA MAR

For many Californians, the making of new homes began, without any irony, in ruins. They were the picturesque ruins of the colonial-era missions that had been melting into the soil from which their bricks and tiles came since secularization by independent Mexico in the 1820s. Anglo newcomers to California at the end of the nineteenth century, enchanted by the idea melancholy decay, saw in the crumbling missions the dreamy romanticism of a Wordsworth or a Tennyson. Whatever else California lacked as a place for its new possessors, at least it had its very own "bare ruined choirs."

What Californians sought in the missions—a union of place, materials, and history—they wanted to see in homes built in the Spanish style, a wish superbly realized in Florestal (now *Isla Mar*), the Hope Ranch estate designed for Mrs. Peter Cooper Bryce by George Washington Smith in 1925–1926.

It was photographed in "ruins" in 2006 while its restoration by Marc Appleton, architect and grandson of the home's first owners, was underway. With Florestal's restoration, a full circle is nearly made—from the preservation movement that led to the Mission Revival style in the late 1880s, through Smith's own cataloging of "golden age" Spanish and Mexican architecture that propelled the Spanish Colonial Revival in the 1920s, to the efforts of preservationists since the 1970s to protect the houses Smith and other contemporary architects designed, which continues today as a new generation of architects questions how to remake the recent past's evocation of another past that never was. Californians of a romantic temperament always look back, and always we see only ourselves amid the ruins.

Florestal, even partly deconstructed, represents one of Smith's most accomplished designs, oriented with panache to the sea, the costal bluff, and the mountains that rise to the north like a green wall. The house of El Greco in Toledo supplied some of the formal elements of Florestal's entry. But the towering, tapering chimney and the crenellations that command one of three patios signal instead a palace on the edge of Sahara. Step through the intervening room, however, and its patio façade is in the circumspect, unornamented style of Spanish classicism (given that the crests of the three window grills are all different). Go through another doorway, and the next facade, animated by a frieze of lozenges in relief, has the easy domesticity of a colonial-era California hacienda.

Much of this eclectic historicism, however graceful, is only a skin over empty space. Underneath the Moorish tiles are ordinary wood studs and metal conduit, like most period houses built in the past hundred years. It would be a mistake to criticize them for their inauthenticity, however. Houses almost always outlive their ironies. That is their revenge on changing taste.

Smith's painterly talent and his familiarity with Post-Impressionist abstraction informed his short but remarkably prolific career as an architect. (He designed more than 100 projects between 1919 and his death in 1930.) At Florestal, rooms and passages do not evoke the dynamics of the building's structure, as a modernist house might, but rather specific volumes of reflected light. Outside, wall surfaces are not a canvas for molded or carved decoration but screens for the movement of shadows that project from corbels, beam-ends, grills, lanterns, and the tracery of tree limbs. Florestal passes through seasonal and hourly aspects of illumination and darkening, something that distinguishes nearly all of Smith's work and something he learned in the famous light of Andalusia.

Waxing and waning shadows, growth and death of the landscaping, the decay of construction materials, and even its eventual ruins are compounded into every building's history. Time's arrow cannot be stopped, even by the best-intentioned restoration.

Like *Casa del Herrero* (page 190), Florestal was filled by its first owners with gatherings from their Mediterranean tours, a small part of the tide of semi-antiques that well-to-do Americans brought back from battered Europe after World War I. Smith made comfortable rooms for them, as he had to for demanding clients. Florestal—caught in a moment of transition among its real and imagined pasts in 2016—shows what Smith put beneath the tapestries and behind the dark furniture: architecture notable for its self-possession as it passes through light and time.

INDEX
OF
HOUSES

THE FRENCH RANCH
Thomas Bollay, architect
Contemporary Spanish Colonial Revival

LOS PAVOS REALES
Wallace Neff, architect
1926

LIBBY STABLES
Wallace Neff, architect
1923

RAVENSCROFT
George Washington Smith, architect
1922

OJO DEL DESIERTO
W. C. Tanner, architect
1926

GUERRA ESTATE
Paul Williams, architect
1927

STRAUSS HOME
Architect unknown
1925

GRAVES HOUSE

RANCHO DE LOS QUIOTES
Designed by original owner, Leo Carillo
1937
www.carlsbadca.go/parks/carillo

VILLA AURORA
Mark Daniels, architect
1928
www.villa-aurora.org

DOLGEN HOUSE
Richard Requa, architect

CASA DEL HERRERO
George Washington Smith, architect

BLACK RESIDENCE
Lillian Rice, architect
1920s

WILK-BURCH HOUSE
Arthur Kelly, architect
1925

HOFER HOUSE
Designed by owner Bret Hofer
Contemporary Spanish Colonial Revival

CASA ROMANTICA
Carl Lindbom, architect
1927
www.casaromantica.org

OGLIVY ESTATE
George Washington Smith, architect
1926

EL BOSQUE
George Washington Smith, architect
1925

ISLA MAR (FLORESTAL)
George Washington Smith, architect
1925

Bibliography

Appleton, Marc. *George Washington Smith: An Architect's Scrapbook*. Los Angeles: Tailwater Press, 2001.

Bueka, Robert. *SuburbiaNation*. New York: Palgrave McMillan, 2004.

Clark, Clifford Edward, Jr. *The American Family Home: 1800–1960*. Chapel Hill, NC: University of North Carolina, 1986.

Cook, S.F. and Tina Skinner. *Architectural Details: Spain And The Mediterranean*. Atglen, PA: Schiffer Publishing, 2005.

———. *Spanish Revival Architecture*. Atglen, PA: Schiffer Publishing, 2005.

———. *California Colonial Homes: Case Studies with Prominent Architects*. Atglen, PA: Schiffer Publishing, 2005.

Dailey, Victoria, Natalie Shivers, and Michael Dawson. *LA's Early Moderns: Art/Architecture/Photography*. Los Angeles: Balcony, 2003.

DeLyster, Dydia. *Ramona Memories: Tourism and the Shaping of Southern California*. Minneapolis, MN: University of Minnesota, 2005.

Deverell, William. *Whitewashed Adobe: The Rose of Los Angeles and the Remaking of its Mexican Past*. Berkeley: University of California, 2004.

Deverell, William, and Greg Hise. *Land of Sunshine: An Environmental History of Los Angeles*. Pittsburgh. PA: University of Pittsburg, 2005.

Dimendberg, David. *Film Noir and the Spaces of Modernity*. Cambridge, MA: Harvard, 2004.

Elias, Judith W. *Los Angeles: Dreams to Reality, 1995–1915*. Northridge, CA: Santa Susana Press, 1983.

Gebhard, Patricia. *George Washington Smith: Architect of the Spanish-Colonial Revival*. Layton, UT Gibbs Smith, 2005.

Hannaford, Donald R. and Revel Edwards. *Spanish Colonial or Adobe Architecture of California*. New York: Architectural Book Publishing Co., 1931.

Heimann, Jim. *California Crazy and Beyond: Roadside Vernacular Architecture*. San Francisco: Chronicle Books, 2001.

Hines, Thomas S. *Irving Gill and the Architecture of Reform*. New York: Monacelli Press, 2000.

———. *Richard Neutra and the Search for Modern Architecture*. Rizzoli International Publications, Inc., New York: 2005.

Hunter, Paul Robinson, and Walter L. Reichardt (editors). *Residential Architecture in Southern California*. Santa Monica: Hennessey & Ingalls, 1998.

Jackson, John Brinckerhoff. *A Sense of Place, a Sense of Time*. New Haven, CN: Yale, 1994.

Kanner, Diane. *Wallace Neff and the Grand Houses of the Golden State*. New York: Monacelli Press, 2005.

Marcus, Clare Cooper. *House as a Mirror of Self: Exploring the Deeper Meaning of Home*. Berkeley: Conari Press, 1995.

Masson, Kathryn. *Santa Barbara Style*. New York: Rizzoli International Publications, 2001.

McClung, William Alexander. *Landscapes of Desire: Anglo Mythologies of Los Angeles*. Berkeley: University of California, 2000.

McMillian, Elizabeth. *California Colonial: The Spanish and Rancho Revival Styles* (Schiffer Design Book). Atglen, PA: Schiffer Publishing, 2002.

———. *Casa California: Spanish-Style Houses from Santa Barbara to San Clemente*. New York: Rizzoli International Publications, Inc., 1996.

Moore, Charles, Gerald Allen, and Donlyn Lyndon. *The Place of Houses*. Berkeley: University of California , 2000.

Neff, Jr., Wallace, ed., David Gebhard, Alson Clark, Wallace Neff. *Wallace Neff: Architect of California's Golden Age* (California Architecture and Architects, No. 22). Santa Monica: Hennessey & Ingalls, 2000.

Neff, Wallace. *Wallace Neff (1895-1982): The Romance of Regional Architecture*. Santa Monica: Hennessey & Ingalls, 1998.

Newcomb, Rexford. *Mediterranean Domestic Architecture for the United States, Twentieth Century Landmarks in Design, Vol. 9* (Acanthus Press Reprint Series). New York: Acanthus Press, 1999.

———. *Spanish-Colonial Architecture in the United States*. Mineola, NY: Dover Publications, 1990.

Ovnick, Merry. *Los Angeles: The End of the Rainbow*. Los Angeles: Balcony Press, 1994.

Peixotto, Ernest. *Romantic California*. New York: Scribner's, 1910.

Poe, Stanley. *Naples: The First Century* (Naples, the City or Red Tile Roofs, the First Century, the Island). Stanley Poe, 2005.

Polyzoides, Stefanos, Roger Sherwood, James Tice. *Courtyard Housing in Los Angeles: A Typological Analysis*. New York: Princeton Architectural Press; 1997.

Robinson, W. W. *Ranchos Become Cities*. Pasadena, CA: San Pasqual Press, 1939.

Roderick, Kevin and J. Eric Lynxwiler. *Wilshire Boulevard: Grand Concourse of Los Angeles*. Santa Monica: Angel City, 2005.

Rodriguez, Richard. *Brown: The Last Discovery of America*. New York: Penguin, 2003.

Rybczynski, Witold. *Home: A Short History of an Idea*. New York: Penguin, 1987.

Starr, Kevin. *Inventing the Dream: California through the Progressive Era*. New York: Oxford, 1986.

———. *Material Dreams: Southern California through the 1920s*. New York: Oxford, 1999.

Zack, Michele. *Altadena: Between Wilderness and City*. Altadena, CA: Altadena Historical Society, 2004.

Diane Keaton would like to thank the following people who were instrumental in getting this book made:
Charles Miers, Douglas Curran, David Morton, and Maria Pia Gramaglia at Rizzoli
for all their support in helping to realize this book. Thanks to our amazing writer D.J. Waldie for his remarkable
essays about the homes included in this book. Thank you to our designer Lorraine Wild, an exceptional,
generous artist and her amazing team for their endless hours of dedication.
Thank you to our photographers, Paul Hester and Lisa Hardaway for their beautiful photographs that brought these
wonderful homes to life. Thank you to Carolyn Barber and Doug Woods for helping keep this project on track.
Most especially, thank you to the following people for sharing their exquisite homes with us:

Diane English and Joel Shukovsky
Rachel Sweet and Tom Palmer
Anne Ramis and Harold Ramis
David Hinshaw
Tracy Conrad and Paul Marut
and all at the O'Donnell House and the
Willows Historic Palm Springs Inn
Gina and Rod Guerra
Peter & Rachel Strauss
Maxine Graves and the late Clifton Graves
Mick Calarco, The City of Carlsbad Recreation
Department, *and all at Leo Carrillo Ranch Historic Park*

The Friends of Villa Aurora
and The Foundation for European-American Relations
Casa del Herrero
Paula and Steve Black
Diane Wilk and Michael Burch
Philip and Karen Ingram
Brett Hofer
Casa Romantica Cultural Center and Gardens
Arthur J. Rice
Joan Kreiss and Roger Perlmutter
Ellen Sarver Dolgen and David Dolgen
Geoffrey Claflin Rusack and Alison Wrigley Rusack

Also, thank you to everyone who opened up their homes to us
but whose homes unfortunately we weren't able to include in this book.
You are an inspiration.
The love and care you exhibit in preserving one of these masterpieces is inspiring.

Susan Drescher-Mulzet and Mark Mulzet
Jim and Ellen Bodas
Dr. and Mrs. Krossnoff
Jim Clark
Henry and Donna Gradstein
Barry Sloane
Eileen Curtis at The Mission Inn
Evally Shlensky
Brad Bell and Colleen Bell
Leonard Hill

David Fincher and Cean Chaffin
John and Helen Seeny
Michael and Lynn Baybek
Helene Gordon
Mr. and Mrs. Peter Lauenstein
Bruce and Soni Friedman
Justine Roddick
Mr. and Mrs. Gavin Herbert
David Schwimmer

To the many others who helped us during this process, we are extremely grateful:

Aileen Comora

Suzanne Neal Perkins

Melissa Birch

Harry W. Kolb

Gwen White

Dirk Sutro

Sally van Haitsma

Debbie Toohey

Elizabeth Puro

Steve Pougnet

Elizabeth Coutier

Catherine Barry

Pamela Regan

Scott Aurich

Sandy McLeod Ryan

Claire Hanssen-Ellingsberg

Richard von Ernst

Matt Boyd

Doug St. Denis

Maureen Murphy

John McIntyre

Tom LeMieux

Stuart M. Campbell

Jody Fine

Emil Alexander

Larry Wild

Chuck Esterly

Kim Perkins

Stephanie Heaton

Noah Hester

Michele Fogelsonger

Catherine K. Stephens

Michael Pierce

Arthur Ollman

Guy Webster

Parker Jackson

John Burnham

Bill Robinson

Marc Appleton

Roger Renick

Scott Wells

Don & Dee at the Old California Store

Christy Walden

Jonathan Gale

John Downer

Mark Hilbert

Martin Newman

Tom Sullivan

Mary Ann Gordon

Steve and Deborah Soukup

Linda Dishman

and the Los Angeles Conservancy

Jim Adams

Ellen DeGeneres

Portia de Rossi

Liz Becker

Allegra Yust Woods

Jim Heimann

Noel Daniel

Jean Parry

John Lofgren

Kay Dalton

Eric Johnson

Steve Carver

Matt Loatman

Maria Llambias

Ryan James

Cricket and Louise at We Wrap

Claudia Gordon

and everyone at Villa Aurora

Everyone at Casa del Herrero

Kimberly Tucker

and everyone at the O'Donnell house

Matt Walker

Carey Kendall

Janice Parente

Sara Willens

David and Lynn Hawkins

Stephen Shadley

Brian Fortman

Michael Gendler

Felecia Brothers

Anne Lopez

Victoria Lam

Robert Ruehlman

Tony Manzella

Rusty Sena

Leslie Sun

319

ISBN: 0-8478-2975-8
ISBN-13: 978-0-8478-2975-0
Library of Congress Control Number: 2007924262

© 2007 Rizzoli International Publications, Inc.
"The Perfect World" (Introduction) © 2007 Diane Keaton
Photography © 2007 Lisa Hardaway and Paul Hester (www.photogypsies.com)
Text (except introduction) © 2007 Donald (D.J.) Waldie

Project editors:
Carolyn Barber and Douglas Woods

Distributed to the U.S. trade by Random House, New York

DESIGNED BY
LORRAINE WILD AND DIANE KEATON
WITH VICTORIA LAM/GREEN DRAGON OFFICE

TYPESET IN VENDETTA BY JOHN DOWNER
INITIALS DRAWN BY JOHN DOWNER

PRINTED AND BOUND IN CHINA

2007 2008 2009 2010 2011/ 10 9 8 7 6 5 4 3 2 1